MW00833887

"New York was no mere city. It was instead an infinitely romantic notion, the mysterious nexus of all love and money and power, the shining and perishable dream itself."

—JOAN DIDION

William J. Hennessey

FIFTH AVENUE

From Washington Square to Marcus Garvey Park

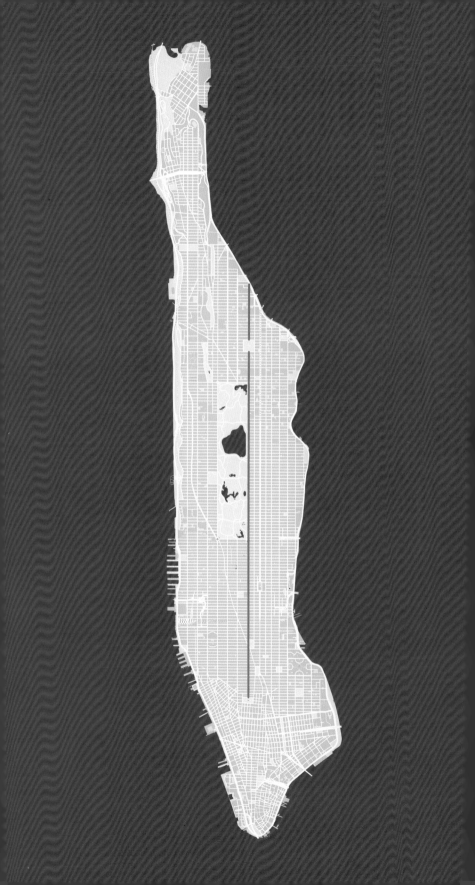

Contents

Preface

Those of us who grew up in the suburbs within easy striking distance of Manhattan tend to remember our early experiences of the city very clearly. Perhaps your parents took you to a Broadway show, or to the American Museum of Natural History to see the dinosaurs, or maybe you remember your first view of the skyline from a ferry crossing the Hudson. For me it was our family's annual pilgrimage to Fifth Avenue that stands out. Every December we would pile into my grandparents' car and head through the Lincoln Tunnel toward a holiday wonderland. Together we would work our way up Fifth Avenue from Altman's to Lord & Taylor, then to Saks, pausing to greet the lions at the New York Public Library before reaching our final goal: the illuminated tree at Rockefeller Center.

Over the years I discovered that there was more to Fifth Avenue than department stores, Christmas windows, and the parades celebrating heroes of many nationalities. In high school, it was the residential elegance of Washington Square that captured my imagination. Later, Fifth Avenue provided a route by which to explore the rich history and architecture of Harlem. In college I was drawn not just to the lions, but also to the reading rooms at the NYPL and to the art collections at the Metropolitan Museum of Art and the Frick Collection. Later still, I discovered the wonderful smaller museums along Museum Mile. At some point it dawned on me that many of the key landmarks that define New York City—Washington Arch, the Empire State Building, the New York Public Library, Rockefeller Center, the Plaza Hotel, and Central Park are, not by coincidence, located along Fifth Avenue. I discovered that Fifth Avenue is a street with a remarkably rich and varied history, one with many aspects and personalities.

This volume is the result. It explores the architecture, history, and still evolving personality of Manhattan's central avenue through a series of walks along the seven miles from Washington Square to the Harlem River. We will discover many of New York's most beautiful and evocative buildings, the circumstances that brought them into existence, and some of the stories that lie behind their facades. *Fifth Avenue* is a book about strolling and looking, about observing and wondering, a book to read at home and a guide to take with you into the streets.

Introducing Fifth Avenue

Fifth Avenue owes its existence to the celebrated Commissioners' Plan of 1811, which laid out the streets of Manhattan Island north of Houston Street on a rigid rectangular grid of east–west streets and north–south avenues. From the start, Fifth Avenue was envisioned as the city's central boulevard, a grand avenue, the "Spine of Gotham." Manhattan's building numbers begin here, stretching out to the east and west.

Fifth Avenue was conceived as Manhattan's premier residential address—at the center of the island, on high ground, and at a safe remove from the industry, noise, and dirt along the river fronts. In 1811, however, the Commissioners' Plan was largely aspirational. Fifth Avenue from Washington Square to 13th Street did not even open to traffic until 1824. The road was extended northward to 42nd Street in 1837 and did not reach its terminus at 143rd Street until 1868. By the 1870s Fifth Avenue was fully paved only as far north as 57th Street. Development proceeded more or less sequentially from south to north.

Living on Fifth Avenue

Fifth Avenue's status as a fashionable place to live shaped its development and evolution. By the 1830s increasing commercial development at the south end of Manhattan pushed prosperous families to relocate ever farther northward in search of peace and quiet. The area near Washington Square was a popular choice. Yet in 1842 when Charles Dickens reported on his visit to New York, he did not even mention Fifth Avenue. Ten years later the lower blocks of the avenue were lined with brownstone mansions—home to what social commentator George Templeton Strong wittily described as "Avenoodles."

Great fortunes were made in the years following the Civil War. As newly wealthy residents moved uptown, they were eager to put their riches on display. By 1870 there were 115 millionaires in Manhattan. Among the first to proclaim personal prosperity with an appropriately grand home was A. T. Stewart, the department store magnate. In 1869 he built a gleaming

A. T. Stewart house, Fifth Avenue and
34th Street, 1869, John Kellum.

Mary Mason Jones houses, Fifth Avenue
and 58th Street, 1869, Robert Mook.

stone palace on the northwest corner of Fifth Avenue and 34th Street. Stewart's house signaled a major shift in taste and style. Instead of brick or brownstone, Stewart built in marble. Rather than restrained Italianate detailing and a simple cornice, Stewart embraced the lushly embellished style of Second Empire Paris, including its signature Mansard roof. The house was the first of an impressive line of Gilded Age mansions that would appear along upper Fifth Avenue in the years to come.

While the Stewart house was rising, social arbiter Mary Mason Jones was erecting her own impressive Marble Row of mansarded mansions on the east side of Fifth Avenue between 57th and 58th Streets. Ten years later, the children of the recently deceased Commodore Cornelius

Caroline Schermerhorn Astor house, Fifth Avenue and 65th Street,
1896, Richard Morris Hunt.

Vanderbilt began construction on a remarkable series of increasingly elaborate houses along Fifth Avenue in the upper 50s. Virtually all of New York's very wealthy soon followed.

The next crucial step in society's northward migration came in 1893 when Caroline Astor (THE Mrs. Astor) abandoned her 34th Street house across from the Stewart mansion and erected a French chateau on the corner of Fifth Avenue and 65th Street. For the next quarter century, dozens of remarkable private palaces were built on along Fifth Avenue facing Central Park and on adjacent streets.

During the 1920s the stretch of Fifth Avenue facing Central Park underwent another transformation as rows of impressive apartment houses replaced many of the mansions. In the same years, an additional group of handsome apartment buildings were erected along the avenue south of 12th Street. It is only on these blocks, facing Central Park or near Washington Square, that, thanks to the benefits of careful zoning, Fifth Avenue has retained its purely residential character.

During the final years of the nineteenth century, the blocks of Fifth Avenue north of Central Park in Harlem were developed as a handsome residential enclave complete with clubs and churches. Brownstone row houses dominated, with small apartment buildings making an occasional appearance. Although today much of the area has been redeveloped, many beautiful houses and historic churches remain, particularly in the blocks near Marcus Garvey Park.

New York as a Shopping Capital

In 1892 the guidebook writer Moses King noted: "All America goes to New York for its shopping." Manhattan's emergence as a retail and wholesale capital was no accident. Long the nation's largest port and the undis-puted center of the needle trades and garment industry, the city remains America's financial center and a key merchandise distribution point.

A. T. Stewart was a pioneer in the emergence of New York as a retail destination. In 1845 he opened his "marble palace" on Broadway just north of City Hall. Not only was Stewart's store architecturally impressive, but his way of selling was innovative. All items were clearly priced. There was no haggling. The sales force was composed largely of helpful young women, and the tone was genteel. Stewart's store was a runaway success, and others quickly followed his example.

Ever larger and more elaborate stores sprung up along the Ladies' Mile on Broadway and Sixth Avenue with restaurants and tea rooms, theaters, skylit rotundas, nurseries, art galleries, and, often, large pipe organs to entertain customers while they shopped. Over time, as transportation infrastructure developed, New York's retail center moved from City Hall to Union Square, then around 1900 to Herald Square, and then to Fifth Avenue.

As new mansions rose along the avenue, churches, clubs, hotels, restaurants, and specialty retailers followed their clients. Tiffany and Company is a good example: the business was established in 1838 on lower Broadway, then New York's prime shopping street. In 1869 Tiffany's moved north to

"Fifth Avenue: The World's Greatest Shopping Street," poster, 1932.

Union Square and then in 1906 to Fifth Avenue and 37th Street. It made a final relocation in 1940 to its present home at the corner of Fifth Avenue and 57th Street. The story of many other major New York retailers is similar. Soon Fifth Avenue was being styled New York's "Via Appia of Opulence" —on a par with London's Bond Street and the Rue de la Paix in Paris—and today, this elegant boulevard is still lined with the flagship stores of American and European luxury brands.

Civic Institutions

With the fortunes that were made in the later years of the nineteenth century came a growing sense of civic responsibility, a desire to make American cities not just utilitarian but beautiful as well. Civic leaders aspired to create broad boulevards, elegant parks, and public buildings of monumental grandeur. Such ordered and beautiful cities would, planners believed, be not just a source of pride, but would promote moral and civic virtue. These ambitions were crystalized by the Chicago World's Columbian Exposition of 1893—a gleaming white city that embodied the era's highest aspirations for urban design.

Architects across America soon embraced the planning principles taught at the Parisian École des Beaux-Arts: symmetry, axiality, and the sequential and harmonious arrangement of interior spaces. Fluent in

Washington Arch, Washington Square, photographed by Samuel Gottscho, 1929.

Rendering of the Fifth Avenue facade of the Metropolitan Museum of Art, McKim, Mead & White, 1906.

the classical vocabulary of architectural forms, they erected museums, libraries, concert halls, clubs, court houses, fountains, and plazas. Through such efforts they and their patrons signaled a new national confidence, a belief that American cities were now the equal of their European counterparts in dignity and elegance.

In New York a very significant number of these landmark structures were built along Fifth Avenue: the Washington Arch, Madison Square, the New York Public Library, St. Patrick's Cathedral, Grand Army Plaza, and the Metropolitan Museum of Art. In the process Fifth Avenue became not just a premier residential address and a fashionable shopping boulevard, but a street of great institutions, beautiful churches, and inspiring monuments. In later years construction of Rockefeller Center embraced much of the same spirit. Today no street in New York can match Fifth Avenue for the range and quality of its public monuments.

Transportation

Real estate development in New York has always been closely linked with access to public transportation. New neighborhoods (the Upper West Side, Washington Heights, Harlem) typically developed only when elevated or subway service arrived, permitting residents to commute easily to jobs in mid- or downtown Manhattan.

Fifth Avenue is one of the very few New York avenues never to have been served by a streetcar line, an El, or a subway. No disruptive subway construction or noisy, unsightly trestles were allowed to disrupt the quality of life. Fifth Avenue merchants and residents pressed hard to keep mass transportation at bay as part of their efforts to ensure that the avenue retained an exclusive, residential character. In 1885 a group of investors led by James A. Roosevelt and William C. Whitney formed the Fifth Avenue Railroad Company with the aim of building a streetcar line along Fifth Avenue from Washington Square to 59th Street. Powerful avenue residents like William Waldorf Astor, Cornelius Vanderbilt, and Chauncey Depew quickly organized the Association for the Protection of the Fifth Avenue Thoroughfare to block the project. They succeeded through lawsuits, political pressure, and a public relations campaign.

As an alternative, the Fifth Avenue Transportation Company was soon founded to offer horse-drawn omnibus service along several routes that closely align with today's buses. By 1907 the company switched to gasoline power and at a time when the standard fare on a New York bus was a nickel, the Fifth Avenue Coach Company charged ten cents. The company prospered and expanded its services throughout Manhattan, into the suburbs, and to other cities; by the 1920s the Fifth Avenue Coach Company was the largest bus operator in the country. In 1962, after a strike and a struggle for control of the company, operations were taken over by the city. Among the casualties were the famous double-decker buses that had been a trademark of the Fifth Avenue Coach Company from the start. The view offered from the top level made them popular not only with locals but with tourists for whom a trip up Fifth Avenue along "Millionaire's Row" was a high point of seeing the sights.

The Fifth Avenue Association

Over the years, few civic organizations in New York have been as influential as the Fifth Avenue Association. In 1907, alarmed by the speed of change along what had long been a quiet residential corridor, a group

Traffic light, Fifth Avenue and 42nd Street, c. 1925.

of residents, property owners, and merchants formed an association to ensure that their street did not lose its distinctive character. Early on, the Association successfully joined with other organizations to press for the adoption of the city's first comprehensive zoning ordinance. Traffic was another area of particular concern. In 1920, to deal with the congestion that was an inevitable result of commercial development, the city installed New York's first traffic signal at the intersection of Fifth Avenue and 34th Street. Two years later the Association sponsored a program to expand the number and upgrade the appearance of the traffic signals to ensure a harmonious fit with their surroundings. The result was a set of seven ornate 23-foot-tall tapering bronze towers decorated with classical motifs and featuring illuminated clocks and bells to sound the hours.

The towers, placed on stone pedestals in the middle of the street, soon became a traffic hazard. The Association brought back Joseph Freedlander, who had designed the original signals, to create a more functional model. The new lights debuted in 1931 as streamlined posts placed on corners, rather than mid-traffic. Each two-light signal was topped with a gilded 17-inch bronze figure of Mercury. Ultimately, 103 of these lights would be installed between 8th and 59th Streets. They would remain beloved fixtures until 1964 when they were replaced. As a further measure to speed the movement of traffic the Association pressed in 1924 for the widening of Fifth Avenue's traffic lanes by reducing the size of the sidewalks, and in 1966 the avenue became one-way southbound.

The Association also secured passage in 1917 of an ordinance to prohibit illuminated or projecting signs along Fifth Avenue. Other major Association initiatives have included successful involvement in efforts to ban traffic from Washington Square Park, to defeat of Robert Moses's plans for a mid-Manhattan expressway, and to create special zoning to regulate the nature of retailing along Fifth Avenue in Midtown. In 1973 the Association was instrumental in the adoption of zoning to limit the height of buildings along Fifth and Park Avenues and to mandate the retention of a uniform street wall. More recently the Association has focused its activities on the Fifth Avenue Business Improvement District stretching from 46th to 61st Streets, managing the evolving mix of businesses, and promoting Fifth Avenue as a shopping and tourist destination.

Today Fifth Avenue is a street of varied and overlapping personalities: a coveted residential address, a prestigious business location, a prime shopping avenue, and a home for many of the city's most notable churches and civic landmarks. At the turn of the twentieth century, nearly every large American city had such a throughfare, a street that was widely recognized as the town's most prestigious address. Boston had Commonwealth Avenue; Cleveland, Euclid Avenue; Chicago, Prairie Avenue; and Washington, Massachusetts Avenue. Most of these streets were developed in a relatively short time beginning in the prosperous years following the Civil War. Nearly all were in serious decline by the 1920s. Fifth Avenue is the exception. It became a fashionable address early on, and over the years, it has demonstrated a remarkable ability to change and adapt. A truly great and vital American avenue, it remains for many Manhattan's address of choice.

Grand Army Plaza, Fifth Avenue and 59th Street, 1904.

West 23rd

East 23rd

West 22nd

East 22nd

West 21st

East 21st

West 20th

East 20th

West 19th

East 19th

West 18th

East 18th

West 17th

East 17th

West 16th

East 16th

West 15th

East 15th

West 14th

East 14th

West 13th

East 13th

West 12th

East 12th

West 11th

East 11th

West 10th

East 10th

West 9th

East 9th

West 8th

East 8th

Waverly Place

West Washington Place

Washington Square Park

West 4th

Washington Square South

Broadway

Fifth Avenue

University Place

Union Square West

South

1. Washington Square Park
2. Washington Square North
3. 29 Washington Square West
4. 37 Washington Square West
5. Vanderbilt Hall
6. Hagop Kevorkian Center for Near Eastern Studies
7. Judson Memorial Church
8. NYU Global Center for Spiritual Life
9. Helen and Martin Kimmel Center for University Life
10. Elmer Holmes Bobst Library
11. Pless Building
12. Brown/Asch Building
13. Silver Center for Arts and Science
14. Washington Memorial Arch
15. Washington Mews
16. 1 Fifth Avenue
17. 2 Fifth Avenue
18. 4–26 East 8th Street
19. New York Studio School
20. Hotel Marlton
21. 10 Fifth Avenue
22. 12 Fifth Avenue
23. 14 Fifth Avenue
24. Brevoort Apartments
25. 24 Fifth Avenue
26. Lockwood de Forest House
27. Ava Apartments
28. Church of the Ascension
A. Ascension Rectory
B. Numbers 20–38 West 10th Street
C. 50 West 10th Street
D. Jefferson Market Courthouse
E. The Second Cemetery of the Spanish and Portuguese Synagogue
F. Numbers 14–26 West 11th Street
G. 18 West 11th Street
H. 12 West 11th Street
29. 39 Fifth Avenue
30. 40 Fifth Avenue
31. 43 Fifth Avenue
32. First Presbyterian Church
33. Church House
34. The Salamagundi Club
I. The Ardea
J. Butterfield House
35. Macmillan Company Building
36. 61 Fifth Avenue
37. 70 Fifth Avenue
38. 72 Fifth Avenue
39. New School University Center
40. The Kensington Building
41. YWCA Building
42. 85 Fifth Avenue
43. 91–93 Fifth Avenue
44. 95 Fifth Avenue
45. Judge Building
46. Pierrepont Building
47. Engine Company 14
48. Constable Building
49. Arnold Constable Store
50. 119–121 Fifth Avenue
51. 129–131 Fifth Avenue
52. 123 Fifth Avenue
53. 134 Fifth Avenue
54. 138 Fifth Avenue
55. Condiac Building
56. 141–147 Fifth Avenue
57. Methodist Book Concern
58. Presbyterian Building
59. 166 Fifth Avenue
60. Sohmer Building
61. Scribner Building
62. Mortimer Building
63. 178–180 Fifth Avenue
64. 182 Fifth Avenue
65. Western Union Building
66. Flatiron Building

Washington Square to Madison Square

By the 1830s Washington Square had become a coveted residential address, but space facing the square was limited. In 1834 landowner Henry Brevoort Jr., whose family farm lay to the north and east, became the first person to erect a mansion on Fifth Avenue itself. His Italianate villa stood until the 1920s at the northwest corner of Fifth Avenue and 9th Street. As others followed his example, a nearly unbroken rows of brownstone townhouses soon lined Fifth Avenue all the way to Madison Square, and the street was recognized as the city's most prestigious address.

However, as Henry James noted with dismay when he returned from England in 1904, the character of the neighborhood changed quickly. The first commercial building on lower Fifth Avenue was erected in 1911, and loft buildings soon replaced houses as residents moved uptown. Many of the remaining mansions were subdivided, converted into rooming houses, or replaced by apartments. By the early twentieth century, formerly sedate Greenwich Village had become a bohemian enclave, a welcoming neighborhood for artists, writers, and radicals. In the years since, the blocks north of Washington Square have regained their exclusivity, albeit tempered by the presence of flocks of students from New York University and the New School.

North of 14th Street the avenue's residential character was compromised early on by commercial development along Broadway to the east and Sixth Avenue to the west. By the 1860s the "Ladies' Mile" shopping district stretched north along Broadway from A. T. Stewart's celebrated department store at 9th Street. In 1878 the completion of the El along Sixth Avenue brought new customers to the district. Fifth Avenue was hemmed in between these two busy retail corridors.

The majority of the buildings between 14th and 23rd Streets took on their current appearance during a twenty-year period of intense redevelopment beginning around 1880. During these years, most private residences along this stretch of Fifth Avenue were replaced by large commercial buildings of remarkably similar height and style. Most of the significant structures were the work of a small number of property developers, dominated by Henry Corn. He and his colleagues worked with a small group of architects, such as Louis Korn and Robert Maynicke. (Maynicke himself designed no fewer than sixteen buildings on Fifth Avenue between 14th and 23rd Streets.) This stretch of the avenue comes to a triumphant conclusion at Madison Square with one of New York's most celebrated landmarks, the Flatiron Building.

❶ Washington Square Park

What is now Washington Square was originally a marshy meadow bisected by the Minetta Brook. In 1642 the Dutch allocated land here to freed slaves, creating Manhattan's first large Black community. The Dutch intended this settlement to act as a buffer between the native tribes on the northern part of the island and the main colony to the south.

In 1797 the City of New York purchased land from the Black farmers for use as a potter's field. Nearly 20,000 bodies lie below Washington Square Park. The city acquired additional land in 1826 and converted the cemetery into a military parade ground. By the mid-1830s, the square had become a fashionable residential quarter.

In 1849 the parade ground was transformed into a 10-acre park. Over the years it has been reconfigured several times to conform to changing fashions in landscape design. A carriage drive, for example, was added in 1870. In 1952 Parks Commissioner Robert Moses unveiled a plan to extend Fifth Avenue southward straight through the park. Community activists, led by Shirley Hayes, Jane Jacobs, and Eleanor Roosevelt, organized the successful opposition. Washington Square's current appearance is the result of a major redesign begun in 2009 by landscape architect George Vellonakis. Today the park is a lively gathering spot for area residents, students from New York University and the New School, street performers, chess players, political demonstrators, and visitors from around the globe.

❷ Washington Square North

This elegant and graceful row of Greek revival townhouses dates to the early 1830s. Although several houses have been demolished and nearly all have been updated and expanded to the rear, the row still maintains the look and feel of early nineteenth-century New York. Henry James's grandmother lived at Number 18, and her house provided the inspiration for *Washington Square*.

The houses to the east of Fifth Avenue, known as "The Row," are particularly well preserved. At his death in 1801, Captain Robert Richard Randall, who owned a 21-acre farm to the north, bequeathed his property for use as a site for "an asylum, or Marine Hospital to maintain and to support aged, decrepit, and worn-out sailors" —the Sailor's Snug Harbor. Instead of building on Randall's land, the Snug Harbor trustees leased the property for development, using the proceeds to erect a handsome campus on Staten Island. The leases to the resulting houses were taken up by many of New York's leading merchants, bankers, and real estate developers. Note the deep front gardens, sturdy stone balustrades, handsome Doric and Ionic porticoes, and the original black and white marble paving that survives in front of Number 5. Many of the houses retain their original cast-iron fences. Today the entire block is controlled by New York University under a 200-year lease from Snug Harbor.

The houses to the west of Fifth Avenue were developed separately and are more diverse in style. Like those to the east, all have been remodeled and extended to the rear. The row is anchored at the center of the block by a double-width mansion and bracketed by newer construction at either end.

Washington Square West

Nearly all the real estate fronting on Washington Square is owned or controlled by New York University. The University has been a presence on the Square since its founding in 1831 and today hosts more than 12,000 students in nearly 100 neighborhood buildings. The west side of the square is filled with apartment houses mostly dating from the 1920s. **29 Washington Square West** ❸ (1926–27; Gronenberg & Leuchtag) features some attractive Gothic details and a handsome entrance canopy. The same firm also designed **37 Washington Square West** ❹. Here the Venetian-inspired terra-cotta balconies and window frames steal the show.

Washington Square South

NYU classroom buildings dominate the south and east sides of the Square, beginning on the southwest corner with **Vanderbilt Hall** ❺ at 40 Washington Square South (1951; Eggers & Higgins). This understated Georgian building with its pleasant, secluded courtyard behind an arched loggia is the home of NYU's Law School.

❻ Hagop Kevorkian Center for Near Eastern Studies

50 Washington Square South

1970–72 · JOHNSON & FOSTER

This cool 1970s exercise in granite geometries is more than a little forbidding on the exterior. But walk into the lobby and you will find yourself transported to a late-eighteenth century merchant's house in Damascus (skillfully interwoven with contemporary architectural elements). Art dealer Hagop Kevorkian donated the room to the Center. Another room from the Damascus house is installed uptown at the Metropolitan Museum of Art.

❼ Judson Memorial Church

54 Washington Square South

1888 (TOWER 1895) · STANFORD WHITE OF MCKIM, MEAD & WHITE

The church's founder, Baptist preacher Edward Judson, sought to create an institution that would serve not only the spiritual but also the educational, social, and physical needs of the Italian immigrants then

flooding Lower Manhattan. With the backing of John D. Rockefeller, Judson commissioned Stanford White to design this refined and elegant structure.

From the start the Judson Memorial Church (named for Edward Judson's father, America's first Protestant missionary) was a blend of church and settlement house, a bold pioneer in addressing progressive social and public health issues of all kinds. Today the church also presents a program of musical, dance, and theatrical performances.

The church building is simple in its massing but rich in detail. A bold pedimented facade faces the square; the auditorium with its graceful row of arches and windows is elevated above a rusticated basement. The basic forms are of Italian inspiration, a little Early Christian, some Romanesque, and a strong dose of the Renaissance. As always with White, the proportions are perfect. There is beautiful yellow Roman brick, intricate terra-cotta detailing, and fine marble and limestone accents. A sumptuous entrance portal on Washington Square South sits between the soaring Romanesque tower and the church proper.

The boxlike church interior is ennobled by majestic, coffered arches on three side and by an open trussed roof supported by finely detailed corbels. Seventeen richly toned stained-glass windows by John La Farge comprise the largest collection of the artist's work remaining in situ. The elegant marble relief sculpture in the baptistry at the east end with its winsome floating angels was carved by Herbert Adams to a design by Augustus Saint-Gaudens.

❽ NYU Global Center for Spiritual Life

238 Thompson Street
2012 · MACHADO SILVETTI

The Center's facade is a curtain wall of quartzite stone panels, perforated to evoke an abstracted image of a growing tree. As it rises, the facade opens to reveal increasingly large windows. Additional windows are hidden behind the lower panels, which screen the entering light. The effect at night when the interiors are illuminated is dramatic, creating an arresting interplay between opacity and transparency, crisp geometry, and the organic patterning.

❾ Helen and Martin Kimmel Center for University Life

60 Washington Square South
2003 · ROCHE DINKELOO

A cool, utilitarian composition that is both NYU's student center and the home of the 860-seat Skirball Center for the Performing Arts. The segmentally arched glass canopy protecting the entry is echoed higher on the facade first in a projecting balcony and then in a two-story bowed window. The glass enclosed penthouse floors slope inward to suggest a traditional mansard roof.

⑩ Elmer Holmes Bobst Library

70 Washington Square South
1965–72 · JOHNSON & FOSTER

NYU's 12-story library dominates the southeast corner of the square. The scale of this cubic mass of red sandstone is overwhelming, and the detailing self-consciously monumental. Inside, however, the soaring atrium is an impressive space.

Washington Square East

This side of the square is dominated by NYU classroom buildings, including the appealing red brick **Pless Building** ⑪ at 80 Washington Square East. Built as the Benedick in 1879 by McKim, Mead & Bigelow, this early apartment building originally included several artist studios. Winslow Homer, John La Farge,

and architect William Rutherford Mead were tenants.

At the northwest corner of Greene Street at 23–29 Washington Place, is the **Brown/Asch Building** ⑫ (1900–01; John Woolley), site of the horrific Triangle Shirtwaist fire. On the afternoon of March 25, 1911, 146 immigrant women lost their lives when a fire broke out in the upper floor loft where they were sewing. Locked stair doors and damaged fire escapes prevented employees from reaching safety. The tragic loss of life led to important changes in New York City's fire safety standards, zoning, and labor regulations.

The remainder of the east side is occupied by NYU's **Silver Center for Arts and Science** ⑬ (1895; Alfred Zucker), home to the university's Grey Art Gallery. This was the site of NYU's original home, a Gothic

Revival building designed by A. J. Davis and erected in 1834. A fragment of the Davis building is preserved in Schwartz Plaza just to the east of the Bobst Library.

⓮ Washington Memorial Arch

1889–95 · STANFORD WHITE OF MCKIM, MEAD & WHITE

On April 30, 1789, George Washington stood on the steps of Federal Hall in downtown Manhattan and was sworn in as our nation's first President. One hundred years later businessman William Rhinelander Stewart, who lived at 17 Washington Square North, felt the anniversary deserved commemoration. He raised private funds to erect a triumphal arch to celebrate the inaugural centenary.

The temporary arch, designed by Stanford White and constructed of wood and plaster, spanned Fifth Avenue just north of Washington Square. It was a tremendous success and funds were quickly raised for a permanent version. White's new arch, 77 feet tall and constructed of white Tuckahoe marble, was dedicated in 1895. Inspired by ancient Roman prototypes, it is a handsome

affair, poised and scholarly.

The arch was originally decorated only with relief carvings, including a crisp frieze and elegant victory figures by Frederick MacMonnies in the spandrels. The energetic eagles are the work of Philip Martiny. Fifteen years later, two statues, *Washington as Commander and Chief, Flanked by Fame and Valor* (1916) by Herman MacNeil and *Washington as President Accompanied by Wisdom and Justice* (1918) by Alexander Stirling Calder, were added to the north side of the arch. The carving was carried out by the Picarilli Brothers, who executed many of New York's turn-of-the-century monuments.

Take a moment to stand directly underneath. Look up at the beautifully designed and executed coffering. Gaze south back into Washington Square Park to the fountain and Judson Memorial Church beyond; then turn and look up Fifth Avenue, where the Empire State Building anchors the vista.

On the east side of Fifth Avenue, just behind the neoclassical houses facing the Square, is the peaceful **Washington Mews.** ⑮ Although open to the public, the Mews has always been a private street. Initially it served as a service alley, accommodating stables and carriage houses for the fashionable residences

facing the park to the south and 8th Street to the north. Over the years, as stables became less necessary, the buildings were converted into residences. In 1916 many were redesigned by architects Maynicke and Franke as artist's studios with stucco facades and inset tile work. By 1939 demand for such artistic dwellings had grown to the point that ten new houses were built on the south side at the west end of the Mews, masquerading as converted stables. In 1950 control of the buildings passed to New York University, which converted the buildings to offices and housing for faculty.

🔟 1 Fifth Avenue

1927 · HARVEY WILEY CORBETT

Corbett's landmark tower rises from a solid base
through multiple setbacks to culminate in a
dramatic central chimney flanked by copper half-
cupolas. This is a building with real Art Deco
glamor—thoroughly modern but retaining the
picturesque aura of a medieval fortress.

🔟 2 Fifth Avenue

1950–52 · EMERY ROTH & SONS

A white brick colossus. Citizen action forced the developer to add the
lower red-brick wing facing the park to suggest the original town houses
that were demolished to allow for the construction of the main building.

At the turn of the twentieth century, 8th Street east of Fifth Avenue was
occupied by aging brick row houses. Many of these had been turned into
rooming houses or converted to commercial use. When the property
leases here and in Washington Mews immediately to the south expired in
1914 the owners, Sailor's Snug Harbor, undertook a major remodeling.
Architect Julius Franke removed the stoops and refaced the buildings at
4–26 East 8th Street 🔟 in stucco with brick trim and Moravian tile
accents to create a picturesque arts-and-crafts enclave. Inside there

were studios and small apartments designed to capitalize on Greenwich Village's emerging identity as an artistic neighborhood.

To the west, adjacent to 2 Fifth Avenue, is the **New York Studio School** ⑲ at 8 West 8th Street. In 1912 Gertrude Vanderbilt Whitney commissioned architect Auguste L. Noël of Noël & Miller convert three town houses into a private art gallery and workspace—the Whitney Studio. The studio included a remarkable sculpted plaster fireplace by Robert Winthrop Chanler, which survives. In 1931 the building became the original home of the Whitney Museum of American Art. Whitney died in 1942. Her museum relocated, and in 1963 the New York Studio School, dedicated to figurative art, moved in. Across the street the recently restored **Hotel Marlton** ⑳ (1900) is a handsome, balanced composition in brick and stone.

10 Fifth Avenue ㉑ is an understated gem. This Gothic townhouse, one of a group of four built in 1848 by Henry Brevoort Jr., features a crenellated cornice, fine window frames and mullions, and stone panels with quatrefoil decoration above the windows on the second floor.

Next door, the eclectic **12 Fifth Avenue** ㉒ (1903; Louis Korn) is among the earliest apartment houses erected along Fifth Avenue. The two-story balconied portico at the center of the facade and the powerful cornice at the seventh floor are

particularly distinctive touches. The nondescript building next door at **14 Fifth Avenue** ㉓ is slated to be replaced by an apartment tower designed by RAMSA.

㉔ Brevoort Apartments

11 Fifth Avenue

1953–65 · BOAK & RAAD

Another glazed-brick giant, built before the area was rezoned to ensure that new buildings did not overwhelm their historical neighbors. The plan is nearly identical to that of 2 Fifth Avenue: a central block with a curved drive is set back from the street and flanked by twin wings. Multiple setbacks begin at the 12th floor. This was the site of the once-famous Brevoort Hotel where in 1927 Charles Lindbergh collected his prize for flying solo across the Atlantic.

24 Fifth Avenue ㉕, on the northwest corner of 9th Street, was built in 1926 by Emery Roth as the Fifth Avenue Hotel. It's an imposing building, enlivened by some Spanish Renaissance embellishments and an elegant entrance canopy.

㉖ Lockwood de Forest House

7 East 10th Street

1887 · VAN CAMPEN TAYLOR

Lockwood de Forest (1850–1932) was a landscape painter and early partner of Louis Comfort Tiffany. He developed a passion for Indian architecture during his honeymoon trip to the subcontinent and utilized teak carvings from a workshop he founded in Ahmedabad in many of

his commissions. Examples are on glorious display in the bay window of this house as well as next door in the entrance and carved address plaque of the **Ava Apartments** ㉗ at 9 East 10th Street (1888; Renwick, Aspinwall & Russell). A complete de Forest interior survives in the Cooper Hewitt Museum uptown. De Forest's house is now the home of NYU's Edgar M. Bronfman Center for Jewish Student Life.

㉘ Church of the Ascension

36 Fifth Avenue

1840–41 · RICHARD UPJOHN; INTERIOR RECONFIGURED 1885– 89, STANFORD WHITE OF MCKIM, MEAD & WHITE

This was the first church to be built on Fifth Avenue and is one of the earliest major New York buildings constructed of brownstone, a material that would enjoy a tremendous vogue in the decades to come. The Ascension congregation moved here after its original home on Canal Street burned in 1839. They chose Richard Upjohn, then at work on Trinity Church, as their architect. Like Trinity, Ascension is a well-proportioned dark sandstone building entered through a central tower. Upjohn took special care with the tower. The progression upward from the entry portal through three lancets and a

28

28

28

tiny transitional window to the
Tudor screen of the bell loft is
assured and satisfying.

The interior, with its gracious
open proportions, creamy stone
walls, and dark wood ceiling,
owes much to a major remodeling
undertaken between 1885 and
1889 by Stanford White. White
commissioned John La Farge to
paint the splendid mural of
the Ascension above the main altar. Unlike most Episcopal churches
of its period, Ascension has no chancel, but La Farge's mural does a
remarkable job of creating an illusion of depth and space on the flat end
wall. The artist also designed several of the stained-glass windows.
The marble and mosaic reredos is the work of Maitland Armstrong, and
the pair of angels supporting a chalice are by Louis Saint-Gaudens,
brother of the more famous Augustus. The beautiful walnut pulpit was
designed by White's partner, Charles McKim.

⬦ 10th and 11th Streets

The blocks to the west of Fifth Avenue along 10th and 11th Streets are among the most handsome and best preserved in the city. They continue to be dominated by nineteenth-century townhouses, all built on land once owned by the Brevoort family.

The **Ascension Rectory Ⓐ**, tucked behind the church at 7 West 10th Street, is filled with personality. Note the crisp Gothic windows treatments, the distinctive projecting central dormer, and the spikey chimney.

Numbers 20–38 Ⓑ are popularly known as "Renwick Row" after their probable designer. Erected between 1856 and 1858, they were among the first rowhouses in the city built without a high stoop.

Both playwright Edward Albee and composer/lyricist Jerry Herman lived for a time in the converted carriage house at **50 West 10th Street Ⓒ**. There is clean, direct Romanesque detailing at the cornice and over the windows. The original sign survives: Grosvenor Private Boarding Stable.

The intersection of 10th Street and Sixth Avenue is dominated by the **Jefferson Market Courthouse Ⓓ** (1874–77; Vaux & Withers; updated in 1967 by Giorgio Cavaglieri). This remarkable High Victorian confection

of polychrome towers, gables, and pinnacles was originally built as the courthouse for New York's Third Judicial District. It makes impressive use of its prominent site and when it was completed in 1877 the *American Architect and Building News* voted it the "fifth most beautiful building in America." After surviving a brush with demolition in the 1960s, it was converted into a branch of the New York Public Library.

The Second Cemetery of the Spanish and Portuguese Synagogue ❸ (72–76 West 11th Street) is a tiny, silent, melancholy oasis, all that remains of what was once a much larger burial ground. Shearith Israel was founded in 1654 as America's first Jewish congregation and remained the only one in New York until 1825. Its first cemetery was on Chatham Square. When burials began here in 1805, this was open countryside. By 1830 continuing development

forced relocation to yet another site on West 21st Street.

The handsome row of Greek Revival townhouses on the south side of 11th Street **(Numbers 14–26)** ❻ were commissioned in 1844 by Henry Brevoort Jr. Five of the houses were gifts to Brevoort's daughters. As on Washington Square North, the houses have high stoops, graceful iron railings, and except those houses that have been altered, fine proportions. The brownstone framing of the entry doors is a distinctive touch.

The house at **18 West 11th Street** ❼ is a new building. On March 6, 1970, after members of the Weather Underground had converted the basement of the original house into a bomb factory, an explosion killed three people and demolished the house. Architect Hugh Hardy designed the replacement. He echoed the basement and attic floors of the neighboring houses but inserted a dramatic two-story angled bay at the center of the facade. The result is a dynamic balance of the old and new, at once respectful and challenging.

In 1889 McKim, Mead & White redesigned an existing townhouse at **12 West 11th Street** ❽ to create an idiosyncratic Parish House for the Church of the Ascension around the corner. The design is an asymmetrical but balanced arts-and-crafts composition in beautiful tan Roman brick with limestone trim around the door and windows.

39 Fifth Avenue ㉙ (1922; Emery Roth) has some notable terra-cotta work on the third floor. Across the way, **40 Fifth Avenue** ㉚ (1929; Van Wart & Wien) is one of the most attractive of the many large apartment buildings erected along lower Fifth Avenue in the 1920s, with a nicely balanced brick-and-stone elevation and a spirited elevator tower. In addition to standard apartments, the building includes several maisonettes, each with its own entry on Fifth Avenue. **43 Fifth Avenue** ㉛ at the northeast corner of 11th Street (1905; Henry Anderson) is a striking Beaux-Arts design complete with a tall, curved mansard roof and a central stack of copper-clad bay windows rising above a very grand entry portal.

㉜ First Presbyterian Church

48 Fifth Avenue

1846 · JOSEPH C. WELLS; SOUTH WING 1893 AND CHANCEL 1918 BY MCKIM, MEAD & WHITE; CHURCH HOUSE, 1960, EDGAR TAFEL

English-born architect Joseph Wells drew on prototypes in Bath and Oxford to create this classic English Perpendicular design. His use of

varying types of sandstone creates an appealing effect of texture and age. A wing was added to the south in 1893 by McKim, Mead & White. The church was expanded again in 1918 by the same architects when popular pastor Henry Emerson Fosdick added the chancel to accommodate his growing flock.

Inside, the nave is broad and low, roofed with plaster groin vaults. The woodwork in dark walnut is especially fine. The warmly chromatic chancel with its altar by Tabor Sears is a particularly pleasing space, adding some ecclesiastical drama to the more low-key nave. In the south wing, the sumptuous Tiffany-designed Alexander Chapel is decorated with Scottish themes and features a fine pipe organ.

In 1960 Frank Lloyd Wright's disciple Edgar Tafel designed a **Church House** ㉝ on the 12th Street side of the sanctuary. The building skillfully combines dark brick and terra-cotta to echo the tonality of the church while the projecting green tile pilasters provide Wrightian accents. Cast quatrefoil panels adapted from the those on the church itself unify the complex and add a suitably Gothic air to the structure.

㉞ The Salamagundi Club

47 Fifth Avenue

1852 · ARCHITECT UNKOWN

This is the only survivor of the rows of nearly identical brownstone mansions that lined Fifth Avenue south of 14th Street in the 1850s. By midcentury, as the wealth and social ambition of New York's leading citizens increased, a new taste for flamboyance and ostentation took hold. The Salamagundi is a perfect exemplar of the new style: high

◇→ 12th Street

24 and 28 West 12th Street are a pair of beautifully proportioned brownstones from 1851–52 built with fine wrought iron and sporting jaunty "eyebrow" cornices over the windows. Across the way at 31–33 West 12th Street is **The Ardea** ❶, built in 1900 to designs by J. B. Snook. It rises to a full ten stories, punctuated along the way with a syncopated series of large and small balconies.

The very handsome **Butterfield House** ❷ at 37 West 12th Street (1962; Mayer, Whittlesley & Glass) elegantly updates the traditional motif of projecting balconies and window bays. A ground-level passage runs through the block to a larger building of similar design on 13th Street.

Further along toward Sixth Avenue at 66 West 12th Street is Joseph Urban's stylish 1930 building for The New School, a bastion of progressive education since its founding as the New School for Social Research in 1919. Urban's flair for the dramatic is evident on the facade with its striking horizonal bands of light and dark brick, punctuated at each floor by continuous strips of windows. The composition rises above a severe entry of polished black stone. Inside is an egg-shaped auditorium with its arched proscenium echoed in a ceiling of concentric bands—a prototype for the later design of Radio City Music Hall. The murals commissioned for the building from Thomas Hart Benton are now at the Metropolitan Museum of Art. A companion set by Jose Clemente Orozco remains in situ.

stoop, lavish door frame with richly carved consoles, rusticated basement, and the overall Italianate detailing. Originally built as the home of coal magnate Irad Hawley, today it houses an artists' club founded in 1871. Louis Comfort Tiffany, John La Farge, and Stanford White were among its members. Public art exhibitions are still regularly held.

③⑤ Macmillan Company Building

60 Fifth Ave

1923–25 · CARRÈRE & HASTINGS WITH SHREVE & LAMB

Built as the American headquarters for the famous British publishing house, 60 Fifth Avenue was purchased in 1962 by the flamboyant publisher Malcolm Forbes. He renovated the building into offices for his eponymous magazine and included galleries for his eclectic collections of Fabergé eggs, Olympic medals, model ships, and toy soldiers. Forbes sold the building to New York University in 2015. The structure is an interesting stylistic blend, reflecting both the Beaux-Arts heritage of Carrère & Hastings and the modernist inclinations of Shreve & Lamb, who went on to design the Empire State Building.

③⑥ 61 Fifth Avenue

2013–14 · ALTA INDELMAN

This stylish rethinking of a classic Fifth Avenue building type presents a narrow facade to the avenue; the main block of the building extends along the side street. There are shops at street level with lofts and apartments above. Indelman's limestone and granite facade rises to a

copper penthouse/mansard. Note how the architect has reduced the perceived height and bulk of a ten-story building by fronting each of the duplex apartments with a single window.

㊲ 70 Fifth Avenue

1912 · CHARLES ALONZO RICH

This was the original headquarters of the NAACP and the home of W. E. B. DuBois's magazine *The Crisis*. In later years it housed a range of important social justice organizations including the League for Industrial Democracy, the Women's Peace Party, the American Fund for Public Service, the American Federation of Teachers, and the Students for a Democratic Society. For many years the National Board of Review of Motion Pictures also had its offices here. Aside from modest changes at street level, the tall, flat slab with its restrained classical detailing retains its original appearance.

㊳ 72 Fifth Avenue

1893; RENOVATED 1913 · ADOLF NAST

In 1917 this classic Romanesque loft building became the headquarters of cigarette maker Philip Morris. Today the building, with its appealing blend of classicizing and Louis Sullivan-inspired ornament, is owned by the New School.

③⑨ New School University Center

63 Fifth Avenue

2010–14 · SKIDMORE, OWINGS & MERRILL

SOM's huge University Center pays frank homage to Joseph Urban's 1930 design for the New School at 66 West 12th Street. Here Urban's striking facade of horizonal bands of light and dark brick, punctuated at each floor by continuous strips of windows, is reinterpreted in aged bronze applied in thin bands. This skin is pierced by a dramatic transparent staircase that zig-zags its way up the building behind faceted glass panels. The openings simultaneously break up the mass of the large structure and offer passersby a glimpse of the activity inside this combination student center and dormitory tower.

④⓪ The Kensington Building

73 Fifth Avenue

1906–7 · SAMUEL SASS

73 Fifth Avenue is typical of commercial structures in these blocks: a two-story base with large display windows gives way to a middle section with floors grouped under a central arch. A decorative crown and strong cornice complete the composition. Only a narrow

facade faces Fifth Avenue. The bulk of the building extends down the side street where real estate is less expensive. The developers of 73 Fifth Avenue lavished an unusual amount of architectural attention on what was a speculative building. Much of the detailing, including the fine copper cornice is intact.

㊶ YWCA Building

7 East 15th Street
1887 · R. H. ROBERTSON

The YWCA was founded in 1870 "to aid self-supporting young women by providing special training in such industries as were adapted to them; to assist them to obtain employment; and to provide opportunities for self-culture." A building on this site was the organization's first home. By 1885 additional space was needed, and thanks to major support from the Vanderbilt and Astor families, this richly textured and dignified Romanesque structure was erected. Rock-faced sandstone on the arcaded ground floor gives way to brick and finished stone above. The building is appealingly vigorous and solid.

The YWCA moved out in 1917. The building was subsequently dubbed "The People's House" and became home to various socialist and labor groups, as well as to the National Woman's Suffrage Party and the Birth Control League of New York. Today 7 East 15th Street houses a Buddhist organization, Soka Gakkai International-USA.

㊷ 85 Fifth Avenue

1900–1901 · LOUIS KORN

If 85 Fifth Avenue seems top heavy, it is because in 1909 the owners tacked on an additional four stories. At street level there is a fine arched entry portal. The brick middle section offers dramatically overscaled stone voissoirs over the windows and Renaissance-inspired terra-cotta embellishments at the eighth and ninth stories. The handsome metal shop front is original.

Early tenants included the publisher Houghton Mifflin, part of an influx of publishers that long made this neighborhood a center for the industry.

The next three buildings were developed by Henry Corn. 87–89 Fifth Avenue (1901–2) is the work of Robert Maynicke. **91–93 Fifth Avenue** ❹❸ (1895–96; Louis Korn) is distinguished by six alluring caryatid figures high up on the facade and by fine Corinthian columns and a projecting cornice above. Maynicke returns at **95 Fifth Avenue** ❹❹, using a now familiar design formula to exploit the advantages of a corner site.

❹❺ Judge Building

110–112 Fifth Avenue

1888–90 · MCKIM, MEAD & WHITE; EXPANDED 1903–4 BY ROBERT MAYNICKE

The Judge Building was commissioned by the land-owning Goelet family. Granite, fine buff-colored Roman brick, and terra-cotta are all marshalled to handsome effect. At the ground level three modest entry portals, accented with delicate carving and oculus windows, are separated by broad display windows. Arched openings above the windows provide a transition from the stone base to the brick midsection.

Just after the turn of the twentieth century, Robert Maynicke undertook several updates to the building. The original crowning arcade was replaced with a cornice, and the arches which topped the grouped windows in the midsection were removed. The careful balance of vertical and horizontal elements and the beautiful patterning on the terra-cotta quoins that enrich the building's rounded corners survive.

Periodical publications were early tenants here, including *Leslie's Weekly* and the satirical *Judge* magazine, which gave its name to the building.

❹ Pierrepont Building

103 Fifth Avenue
1895 · LOUIS KORN

A wealth of classically inspired terra-cotta ornament enriches this narrow, light brick building. The composition may be a bit disjointed, but each section offers something new and interesting. The building is named for politician and U.S. Attorney General Edwards Pierrepont whose house formerly occupied this site.

❹ Engine Company 14

14 East 18th Street
1894–95 · NAPOLEON LE BRUN & SONS

Volunteer fire companies in New York were abolished in 1865 when the city established a professional force. In 1878 the young but ambitious Fire Department began a major building program, and Napoleon Le Brun was hired as chief architect. Between 1878 and 1894 he designed 42 firehouses around Manhattan.

The buildings follow the same basic formula: fire engine and horses on the ground floor, accommodations for the firemen above, linked together by the celebrated brass pole. Le Brun's designs are unabashedly eclectic in style, but all reflect the Department's determination to ensure that its buildings were distinctive civic ornaments.

For Engine Company 14, Le Brun provided a symmetrical, three-story structure in buff brick above a polished granite base. Beautiful terra-cotta ornament, inspired by Italian Renaissance examples, lends the building its flair.

④⑧ Constable Building

109–111 Fifth Avenue
1894–95 · WILLIAM SCHICKEL

④⑨ Arnold Constable Store

113–115 Fifth Avenue
1876 · GRIFFITH THOMAS

Aaron Arnold opened his first store in Lower Manhattan in 1825; the company name changed to Arnold Constable & Company following the marriage of his daughter to James Mansell Constable, an employee who became a partner in 1842. In 1868 with the emergence of Union Square as retail center, the firm hired Griffith Thomas to build a new store at 881–887 Broadway. Business was brisk, and in 1876 the store was extended west along 19th Street to Fifth Avenue. This facade echoes that of the main front on Broadway except that it is executed in cast iron. With its bold mansard roof and richly sculptural facade, the building is

an example of American architectural taste in the decade following the Civil War when designs inspired by the Paris of Napoleon III were in vogue.

The dry goods trade was a lucrative one for the Constable family, and they invested their profits in real estate. In 1893 Henrietta Constable, granddaughter of Aaron Arnold, purchased the lot at the corner of Fifth Avenue and 18th Street and built 109–111 Fifth Avenue as an investment property. It is a first-class building: fine materials, a carefully composed facade, and elegant understated detailing.

The Constable Building was long a favored office location for architects, including Cass Gilbert, Henry Bacon, Robert Maynicke, and Schickel himself.

⑤⓪ 119–121 Fifth Avenue

1905–6 · JOHN H. DUNCAN

⑤① 129–131 Fifth Avenue

1902–3 · R. H. MACDONALD COMPANY

These striking and substantial buildings are the outgrowth of another retail success. Lord & Taylor's main store on Broadway was enjoying enormous popularity, and the firm needed additional space. These buildings are the result. At 119 a vigorously rusticated base is surmounted by a dark four-story central window stack topped by an arch with a lions-head keystone. The attic story is richly detailed with classical motifs in terra-cotta.

Down the block at 129, the architects have grouped their floors under segmental arches accented with bold quoins and prominent keystones. Notice how the size of the window groups and the richness of the decorative accents diminishes as the building rises. A crisp dentilled cornice is carefully aligned with the building to the north. Lord & Taylor would soon follow the retail migration uptown, opening their final store at 39th Street and Fifth Avenue in 1914.

In 1886 Henry Hardenbergh applied this stylish cast-iron shop-front to a former brownstone at **123 Fifth Avenue** 🅱. Such facades with broad planes of glass framed in iron and enriched with decorated spandrels were a popular Parisian motif quickly adopted in New York. Here the gilded grotesque mask and flanking griffins bring the design to life.

🅱 134 Fifth Avenue

1853/1895 · CHARLES T. BEHRENS

🅱 138 Fifth Avenue

1847/1919 · LORENZ WEIHER

Both buildings began life as brownstone residences. As the character of Fifth Avenue shifted, they were converted to commercial use. Number 134 retains its late nineteenth-century cast-iron front. Buildings like these (and particularly the small structure between them) are often called "tax payers" —minimal buildings that generated just enough income to allow the owners to pay the property taxes on their land. Owners frequently acquired and retained them in the hope that rising land prices would lead to a lucrative sale to a developer. Here that sale never happened.

55 Condiac Building

139 Fifth Avenue

1893-94 · ALFRED ZUCKER

Handsome brickwork and understated Renaissance detailing rise above a modern shop front to give the Condiac Building a quiet authority.

56 141–147 Fifth Avenue

1891–1900 · ROBERT MAYNICKE, HENRY EDWARDS FICKEN

The three south bays of the facade are by Robert Maynicke, working again for Henry Corn. But the building's dramatic personality did not emerge until 1899 when a new owner hired Henry Ficken to undertake a major expansion. Ficken adopted Maynicke's original elevation, but spiced things up with an elaborate new entry embellished by a large oculus with swags and garlands. He added a rounded corner at 21st Street and placed a prominent cupola at the top. That cupola, along with the lush ornamentation, richly plastic facade, and the projecting corner balcony make 141–147 Fifth Avenue a striking landmark.

57 Methodist Book Concern

148–152 Fifth Avenue

1888-90 · EDWARD HALE KENDALL

58 Presbyterian Building

154–158 Fifth Avenue

1894-95 · JAMES B. BAKER OF ROWE & BAKER

Large buildings belonging to two mainstream Protestant denominations face each other across 20th Street. Because of the number of religious organizations represented along this stretch of Fifth Avenue,

the blocks were once dubbed "Paternoster Row."

The Methodists' building is a symmetrical composition featuring beautifully laid red brick set off by contrasting stone trim and rich Renaissance detailing above a solid rusticated ground level. The decorative work throughout is crisp, and the twin chimneys flanking the dormer are a particularly successful finishing touch. Built by the church as the headquarters for its education and publishing efforts, there was also rental space. Early tenants included the architect Bruce Price and the Abingdon Press.

Across the way, the Presbyterians also favored arch-topped stacked windows as a key motif for their limestone office building. The best details are at the top, where loosely French Renaissance gabled dormers pierce a hipped roof set above the cornice. In addition to housing the offices of an active missionary program, the Presbyterian Building also offered rental space. Early tenants included the piano manufacturer Knabe, the publisher Little Brown, and *Vogue* magazine. There were several architectural firms as well, including Baker himself and York & Sawyer.

❺❾ 166 Fifth Avenue

1899–1900 · PARFITT BROTHERS

When long-time property owner Margaret Hardenbergh Budd moved uptown, she replaced her mansion with this Northern Renaissance–style commercial building. The ground floor has been completely remodeled, but up above the building is full of personality. The spirited decorative

detailing on the pilasters is only a prelude to the vigorous treatment of the central gable with its deep oculus window and shell cresting. The architects are better known for their domestic and ecclesiastical work in Brooklyn than for Manhattan loft and office structures.

60 Sohmer Building

170 Fifth Avenue

1897–98 · ROBERT MAYNICKE

The cupola makes all the difference. The style here is less exuberant than at 141–147 Fifth Avenue, but the golden dome resting on two stacked octagonal baroque drums is equally eye catching. The building takes its name from the Sohmer Piano Company, an early tenant along with the architectural firm of Cram, Goodhue & Ferguson.

61 Scribner Building

153–157 Fifth Avenue

1893–94 · ERNEST FLAGG

Ernest Flagg, a French-trained American architect, is best known for his elegant townhouses and for his work for the Singer Sewing Machine

Company. Here Flagg provided Scribner's with a combination office and shop building that fully embraced the design principles of the École des Beaux-Arts: a strong central axis, symmetrical massing, balanced vertical and horizontal articulation of the of the facade, and restrained use of classical motifs. The suave cast-iron screen framing the shop windows at ground level is an elegant Parisian touch. In 1913 Scribner's moved north, and Flagg designed a new building for the firm on Fifth Avenue at 48th Street. Flagg's mansion for Charles Scribner (his brother-in-law) is on East 66th Street.

62 Mortimer Building

159–161 Fifth Avenue

1861 · GRIFFITH THOMAS

Avoiding fashionable bombast, Thomas designed an elegantly understated Italian palazzo in light sandstone over a classically detailed ground floor in cast iron. In 1912 the roof was raised and an attic floor inserted. The Mortimer Building, which stretches the depth of the block to Broadway, was among the first commercial structures to rise on Fifth Avenue. Today, in a sign of the times, a Harry Potter store occupies the ground floor.

63 178–180 Fifth Avenue

C. 1862 · ARCHITECT UNKNOWN

These two connected houses were built just as the character of Fifth Avenue was beginning its transition from residential to commercial. The basic design of the buildings is the same, but at some point the

owner of the south building enriched the window detailing and added a pedimented cornice. His neighbor opted for understatement.

Next door **182 Fifth Avenue** ❻❹ (1858/1871) is another example of resourceful updating. Built as a standard four-story brownstone dwelling, the building was given a new cast-iron facade and converted to commercial use.

❻❺ Western Union Building

186 Fifth Avenue

1883 · HENRY J. HARDENBERGH

Hardenbergh designed this Queen Anne style building for Western Union, which in pre-telephone days maintained more than 100 branch telegraph offices around the city. The architect made the most of a prominent site. Dark-red brick, gray stone, and terra-cotta give the building far more visual impact than its relatively small size would lead one to expect.

❻❻ Flatiron Building
(Fuller Building)

173–185 Fifth Avenue

1901–3 · D. H. BURNHAM & CO.

Verbal descriptions of the Flatiron Building do not do it justice: a tall triangular tower designed in the classic three part-formula (base, shaft, capital) and ornamented in a loosely French Renaissance style. This

account does nothing to capture the either the extraordinary drama and dynamism of the building or its remarkable taut, compressed energy. The Flatiron has often been likened to a great ocean liner sailing up Fifth Avenue. Few buildings anywhere have inspired so many painters and photographers.

Filling a tight triangular parcel of land, the building walls rise straight up from the lot line. To the east and west the broad, sheer wall planes converge at a northern apex that is only six feet wide. The building's height (23 stories) and its arresting thinness create extraordinary almost vertiginous drama. In addition to the sculptural drama of its form, this is a building of great ornamental subtlety. Every square inch of the surface is covered with embellished terra-cotta panels. The carefully calibrated repertoire of designs brings the flat wall surfaces to life. Note how on each of the sides Burnham has incorporated three slightly protruding bays to break up what might otherwise be static slabs of masonry. And don't overlook the perfectly scaled cornice or the spirited loggia with its vigorous detailing just below.

This is also a building of great ornamental subtlety. Every square inch of the surface is covered with embellished terra-cotta panels. The carefully calibrated repertoire of designs brings the flat wall surfaces to life.

The Flatiron was erected by a leading Chicago construction firm, the George A. Fuller Company, as its New York headquarters. It was the first tall building north of 14th Street, utilized the latest in steel frame technology, and was at the time among the tallest in the city. The small steel and glass pavilion at street level at northern tip was added against the architect's wishes. Today it is a site for periodic art exhibitions.

West 42nd

East 42nd

East 41st

51

52

East 40th

West 40th   C B   A   50
                               48

49   47   East 39th

West 39th
                45
                      46
43   44
      42   East 38th

West 38th

41   40   East 37th

West 37th

39   38
37   36

West 36th   East 36th

35

West 35th   East 35th

West 34th   34   33   **East 34th**

32

West 33rd   30   East 33rd

31   29

West 32nd   28
           27   East 32nd
      26

West 31st   23
      25   22   24   East 31st
           21

West 30th   19   20   East 30th
      18   17

West 29th   16   East 29th

15
14   12
West 28th   11 10   13   East 28th
      9

West 27th   East 27th

7   8
6

West 26th   East 26th

5
4

West 25th   East 25th

2

3

West 24th   East 24th

1

West 23rd   **East 23rd**

Broadway

Fifth Avenue

Park Avenue

Madison Avenue

Park Avenue South

Lexington Avenue

6th Avenue

CHAPTER 2

Madison Square to the New York Public Library

The Commissioners' Plan of 1811 set aside a vast plot of land between 23rd and 34th Streets as a parade or military drill field. As Manhattan developed, the parade was repeatedly reduced in size, and in 1837 the city designated the remaining acreage to the east of Fifth Avenue as Madison Square.

In 1856 Amos Eno opened the Fifth Avenue Hotel at the corner of 23rd Street. Its location at what was then the northern edge of the developed city made the project a risky real estate venture, but the hotel quickly became a social and business anchor. Other high-end hotels and restaurants clustered nearby, including Delmonico's, which moved uptown on Fifth Avenue from 14th Street to 26th Street i n 1876. The opening of the original Madison Square Garden in 1879 at the corner of Madison Avenue and 26th Street established the square as the center of Manhattan's entertainment district. The prestigious character of the neighborhood was secured in 1890 with the opening of McKim, Mead & White's celebrated new Garden on the same site. Madison Square's civic importance was dramatically highlighted in 1899 when it became the focus of a national celebration welcoming Admiral George Dewey home from his triumph at the Battle of Manila Bay. A richly decorated triumphal arch was temporarily erected across Fifth Avenue at 24th Street for the occasion. A similar arch was erected on the same spot in 1918 to welcome General Pershing back from France at the end of the World War I. In the years that followed, pressure from commercial development along Fifth Avenue brought about a change in the neighborhood's character. By the early twentieth century, townhouses had largely disappeared from what is today called NoMad. The entertainment district soon migrated up Broadway to Times Square, leaving the stretch of Fifth Avenue between 23rd and 34th Streets as a commercial corridor.

The next stage of the avenue's evolution unfolded at its intersection with 34th Street. In 1827 William B. Astor purchased the block on the west side of Fifth Avenue between 33rd and 34th Streets as an investment. In 1856 his sons William B. Astor Jr. (and his socially formidable wife, Caroline) and John Jacob Astor III moved north from Astor Place and built two sober, conservative mansions on the block. In 1890 William Waldorf Astor (son of John Jacob) demolished his Fifth Avenue house and moved to England. He redeveloped the site, hiring Henry Hardenbergh to design the Waldorf Hotel. Life next door in the remaining Astor household became distinctly less pleasant, and in 1897 it too was demolished to make way for the competing Astoria Hotel. Family differences, long simmering, were patched up, and the two hotels were linked to function as one. With 1,300 rooms and 40 luxuriously appointed function spaces, the Waldorf-Astoria was at the turn of the century New York's most celebrated hostelry.

Not surprisingly, high-end retailing arrived quickly in the wake of the hotel's opening. By 1905 Tiffany, Gorham, Reed & Barton, and Benjamin Altman had all relocated their stores nearby, and the formerly residential blocks of Fifth Avenue north of 34th Street became the nation's premier shopping district.

As New York's major dry goods stores moved northward, their suppliers inevitably followed. Altman's opening on Fifth Avenue was a catalyst for garment manufacturers to relocate to the blocks nearby. Merchants became concerned that their clients and the garment workers were a bad mix and that manufacturing would depress property values in the now up-scale neighborhood. The Fifth Avenue Association stepped in, securing special provisions in the city's 1916 Zoning Resolution that established districts across Manhattan to regulate development. Through the Association's efforts, the area from 33rd to 59th Streets between Third and Seventh Avenues was placed off-limits to manufacturing. Manufacturers, already pressed by the high rents near Fifth Avenue, settled on the blocks west of Seventh Avenue, north of the new Pennsylvania Station and south of Times Square where rents were lower and where buildings could be erected specifically to meet their needs.

The retail exclusivity of the blocks north of 34th Street was short lived. Woolworth's opened a store on Fifth Avenue and 40th Street in 1917 and other chains followed. Then in 1929 the Waldorf-Astoria was demolished to make way for the Empire State Building. Today the great department and clothing stores have closed, and the specialty retailers have moved north. This stretch of Fifth Avenue is occupied by office and apartment towers and by related street-level shops and eateries. The next major intersection at 42nd Street was long dominated by the Croton Distributing Reservoir. The block-long, 50-foor-high, Egyptian-style reservoir opened in 1842 as a key component in the city's new water supply system. It was demolished in the 1890s to make way for one of New York's greatest civic buildings: the New York Public Library.

❶ 200 Fifth Avenue

1909 · MAYNICKE & FRANKE

Just north of the Flatiron Building, the west side of Fifth Avenue is occupied by 200 Fifth Avenue, once the site of the celebrated Fifth Avenue Hotel. Today the building houses the Italian food emporium Eataly, but it was for years New York's Toy Center, providing office and showrooms for the manufacturers of everything from dolls to electric trains. Out front stands a golden sidewalk clock. Erected in 1909, it is still going strong.

Ahead is the small triangular park that marks the intersection of Broadway and Fifth Avenue. This is **Worth Square** ❷. The obelisk (1857; James Goodwin Batterson) honors General William Jenkins Worth, who served in the War of 1812, the Seminole Wars, and the Mexican American War. The general also gave his name to Worth Street in Lower Manhattan and to Fort Worth, Texas.

❸ Madison Square Park

After a decade of drainage and grading work, this six-acre park opened in 1847, named for the Madison Cottage, a famous roadhouse that stood at the corner of 23rd Street and Fifth Avenue. Since the 1870s Madison Square Park has been a welcoming home not just to strollers but to public sculpture. The torch from the Statue of Liberty was on view here

from the centennial year of 1876 to 1884 as part of an effort to raise funds for the construction of the statue's pedestal. Today the park's sculptures largely celebrate politicians.

At the north end is the stirring group dedicated to Admiral David Glasgow Farragut by Augustus Saint-Gaudens and Stanford White (1881). The figure of Farragut is stalwart and filled with energy. He stands on an exedra that invites visitors to approach. The reliefs on the base, *Courage and Loyalty*, are almost art nouveau in their delicacy, an unwavering upright sword at the center floats above the abstracted waves in the background.

The Park is managed by the Madison Square Park Conservancy, a public/private partnership that maintains the landscape and presents lively programming. Since 2004 the Conservancy has commissioned an ongoing series of public art installations by contemporary artists including Martin Puryear, Antony Gormley, Teresita Fernández, and Maya Lin.

❹ Lincoln Trust Building

204 Fifth Avenue
1914 · C. P. H. GILBERT

Despite the loss of its cornice and of a projecting balcony, the Lincoln Trust Building retains much of its original symmetrical classical dignity. 204 Fifth Avenue is an unusual building for Gilbert, who is far better known for his domestic work.

❺ Cross Chambers Building

210 Fifth Avenue
1901–2 · JOHN B. SNOOK & CO.

A two-story shopfront gives way at the third level to an elegant shallow balcony and then to a dramatic stack of metal-clad bay windows flanked by recessed panels with dentilled borders. There is a curved mansard and a handsome copper-clad dormer up top. The building extends westward through the block to Broadway where it presents a nearly identical elevation.

The lower floors were initially the home of the English leather-goods company Mark Cross. Bachelor apartments, complete with meal and maid service, occupied the upper floors. Within fifteen years, following its clients, Mark Cross moved to new quarters farther north, and the apartments were converted to commercial lofts.

⑥ Croisic Building

218–220 Fifth Avenue

1910–12 · FREDERICK C. BROWNE

A fine Gothic portal faces Fifth Avenue. Up above at the third level is some spirited terra-cotta, including armorial shields with fleur-de-lis and eagles. The building finishes with a splendid copper mansard.

Next door, **222 Fifth Avenue** ❼ is a commercial building handsomely converted from a mid-nineteenth-century dwelling (1912; John C. Westervelt).

⑧ Brunswick Building

225 Fifth Avenue

1906–7 · FRANCIS H. KIMBALL
AND HARRY E. DONNELL

The designers of this imposing structure effectively deploy rich red brick and contrasting stone trim to play off each other. Stone balconies and terra-cotta window surrounds punctuate the eighth and ninth levels. An iron balcony wraps the building at the eleventh floor. The composition finishes with a strong crowning cornice and more terra-cotta ornament. Built as a loft and office building on the site of the former Brunswick Hotel, 225 Fifth Avenue has been converted to apartments.

❾ 236–238 Fifth Avenue

1907 · BUCHMAN & FOX

A solid, understated, loft building distinguished by its handsome iron shop front.

❿ 242 Fifth Avenue

1885 · GEORGE HARDING

Another mid-nineteenth-century private residence transformed with great style into a store and lofts through the addition of a cast-iron facade. The pediment, somewhat improbably, seems to float unsupported by traditional columns. Much of the fenestration is modern, as is, of course, the ground floor.

⓫ 246 Fifth Avenue

1889 · JOHN E. TERHUNE

This is one of the earliest commercial structures along this section of Fifth Avenue. It has suffered a good deal over the years, but the stacked metal-clad bay windows under relieving arches at the corner are an

appealing touch. They lighten the visual weight of the wall just where one would expect it to be most solid. A recent restoration has given the building fresh life and rescued it from the sad fate of George B. Post's much-mauled **251 Fifth Avenue** ⑫ diagonally across the intersection.

⑬ Historic Lamp Post

Southwest corner of Fifth Avenue and 28th Street

New York's first decorative lamp posts were erected by Thomas Edison along Fifth Avenue beginning in 1892. This rare survivor is a revised version of the Edison original, the so-called Type 24 Twin, that was widely used in the early twentieth century. Nearly all these posts were replaced by 1965 with a sleek new Cobra-headed model designed by Donald Deskey. Many of those have in turn been updated or, north of 34th Street, replaced with a new design. Additional historic designs, including the famous 1900 Bishop's Crook post and the long-armed Covington design, appear along Fifth Avenue farther north.

⑭ Second National Bank
(Fifth Avenue Hotel)

250 Fifth Avenue

1907–28 · MCKIM, MEAD & WHITE

250 Fifth Avenue continues McKim, Mead & White's long-standing preference for designs based on Italian Renaissance models. The original bank was built in three stages, with the core building extended to the north in 1913 and westward in 1928. Today the bank is being restored as the entrance pavilion for a new 24-story hotel tower to the west on 28th Street designed by PBDW Architects and Perkins Eastman.

⓯ 256 Fifth Avenue

1893 · ALFRED ZUCKER AND
JOHN EDELMAN

A wild variety of geometric and organic terra-cotta decoration and Moorish arches cover nearly the entire facade. This strikingly exotic design was commissioned by Charles Baudouine, a successful furniture designer and decorator turned real estate developer.

⓰ 261 Fifth Avenue

1928–29 · BUCHMAN & KAHN

The splendid multicolored terra-cotta detailing here, perhaps influenced by Frank Lloyd Wright, is the work of Ely Jacques Kahn, one of New York's great art deco designers. Stylish abstracted trees embellish the facade pilasters and panels above the main entrance step back and down to draw you in. The lobby is a visual feast: a gilded ceiling, art deco lighting fixtures, and a geometric terrazzo floor.

The vacant lot at the southwest corner of Fifth Avenue and 29th Street is slated to be the home of 262 Fifth Avenue, a 60-story supertall apartment building designed by the Russian firm Meganom.

⓱ Church of the Transfiguration
("The Little Church Around Corner")

1 East 29th Street

1849–50 · ORIGINAL ARCHITECT UNKNOWN; LYCHGATE (1896) AND RECTORY, FREDERICK CLARKE WITHERS; LADY CHAPEL (1906), MORTUARY CHAPEL (1908)

It is easy to miss this Episcopal church complex. A year after the congregation was founded in 1848, work began on the present building, set back from the street in the manner of an English country church. The determinedly modest ensemble grew in sections over the years and is charmingly jumbled and picturesque.

The church has long ties to New York's theatrical community. Its nickname dates to 1870 when the priest at the Church of the Atonement on Madison Avenue refused to bury the actor George Holland and suggested that the family try "the little church around the corner." The event is memorialized in a stained-glass window in the nave. Other windows include one of Edwin Booth by John La Farge.

🔟 Marble Collegiate Church

275 Fifth Avenue

1851–54 · SAMUEL A. WARNER

The Collegiate Church of New York was founded in 1628—four years after the colony of New Amsterdam—as a new-world branch of the Dutch Reformed Church. Today the Collegiate Church has four outposts in Manhattan, and this is the largest. Dr. Norman Vincent Peale was the Senior Minister here for 52 years.

The choice of white Tuckahoe marble was a significant investment, but it ensured that the building held its own with mansions and clubs that lined the avenue in the mid-nineteenth century. The focus of Warner's composition is a tall central tower with a pointed spire embellished with simplified Romanesque and Gothic motifs.

⑲ Holland House

276 Fifth Avenue
1891–99 · GEORGE EDWARD
HARDING AND WILLIAM T. GOOCH

When it opened, this was one
of New York's most luxurious
and fashionable hotels. The
reserved Renaissance dignity of
the exterior belied the opulent
interiors: lavish materials,
historic detailing, paintings,
tapestries, mirrors, marble, and gilt ornament modelled on the interior
of Holland House, a private mansion in London. Hotel competition in this
neighborhood was stiff, however, and the exclusivity of the Holland House
lasted only until the Waldorf Hotel opened three blocks north in 1893.

The institution of prohibition in 1919 and the continued northward
migration of the fashionable were death blows to the Holland House. In
1920 it was converted to loft and office use. Today, except for the loss of
a fine portico facing Fifth Avenue, much of the original exterior remains
intact. The interiors are long gone.

⑳ 277 Fifth Avenue

2016–19 · RAFAEL VIÑOLY

At 55 stories, this is the tallest residential
building on Fifth Avenue. Sleek and
assertively vertical in its articulation, the
facade is animated by recessed open
terraces set at varied intervals in the glass.

㉑ The Wilbraham

282 Fifth Avenue
1888–90 · D. & J. JARDINE

The Wilbraham was built to serve the city's population of single men.
Designed as apartment hotel, individual units had no kitchens and

residents dined together on the eighth floor. The Wilbraham was one of several similar establishments built when this stretch of Fifth Avenue, close to clubs and theaters, was a desirable address for ambitious young professionals.

On the exterior, the rich combination of red brick, brownstone, and cast iron with distinctive Romanesque detailing is sober but luxurious, and the quality of the carving is unusually fine. Take time to enjoy the rusticated ground floor and entry portal, the treatment of the colonettes and carved panels surrounding the windows, and the vigorous detailing of the cornice beneath the copper mansard.

Next door to the Wilbraham, **286 Fifth Avenue** ㉒ has a fine Beaux-Arts two-story shop front. **Le Meridien** ㉓ at 292 Fifth Avenue (2020–22; Gene Kaufman) is a 21-story hotel and residence building in bright white brick enlivened by different bonding patterns.

Across the street at 295 Fifth Avenue is the **Textile Building** ㉔, erected in 1920 to serve the fabric community. Note the bronze relief medallion of a mechanical loom over the entrance. The building is currently being renovated for mixed use, including the addition of a two-story penthouse.

㉕ Hotel Wolcott

4 West 31st Street

1902–4 · JOHN DUNCAN

The Wolcott competed with the Aberdeen, Holland House, and the Waldorf-Astoria. These hotels were cities in themselves, offering every imaginable comfort and service for both travelers and permanent residents. They frequently incorporated the latest technology (electric light, telephones, rudimentary air conditioning, elevators) and were the center of much of the city's social life. Architects worked hard to differentiate their hotel buildings from nearby commercial structures, embracing quality materials, overscaled Beaux-Arts decorative details, dormered mansard roofs, and prominent entry portals.

At the Hotel Wolcott, John Duncan, best known as the architect of Grant's Tomb, used pink brick, limestone trim, bronze railings, and bold Beaux-Arts embellishments to dramatic effect. The marquee is obviously new, but the portal with its dramatic rustication and overscaled keystone above a huge stone shield with putti in the tympanum are original. Inside, the lobby is even more lush. Still functioning as a hotel, the Wolcott has been home to a variety of celebrities from Isadora Duncan to Doris Duke. Fiorello LaGuardia held his 1938 mayoral inaugural ball here.

303 Fifth Avenue ㉖ (1909; Buchman & Fox) is a well-detailed early twentieth-century retail and loft building notable as the original home of the famous FAO Schwarz "Toy Bazaar." Next door the facade of **307 Fifth Avenue** ㉗ (1928; William Hohauser) is enlivened with energetic art deco panels.

㉘ Rock Building

315 Fifth Avenue

1906–7 · MAYNICKE & FRANKE

This narrow slab was built by successful merchant tailor Matthew Rock in partnership with the developer Henry Corn. The architect was Corn's favorite: Robert Maynicke. The lower floors were specially designed for their first tenant, Brentano's book shop. Above, the central section is unremarkable, but the treatment of the top three floors with three-window clusters crowned by broken pediments over a richly carved garlanded cornice is distinctive. Today this corner is at the heart of Manhattan's Koreatown, which is centered on the 32nd Street between Sixth and Madison Avenues.

㉙ Reed & Barton Building

320 Fifth Avenue

1904–5 · MAYNICKE & FRANKE

Another project of developer Henry Corn, this time in partnership with heiress Mary Bell, whose mansion stood on the site. The anchor tenant of the new building was the silversmith and jeweler Reed & Barton, which moved here from Union Square. This building put the firm in close proximity to its rivals Gorham and Tiffany, which had also recently moved north.

320 Fifth Avenue has all the now-familiar hallmarks of a Maynicke & Franke project: elegantly detailed shop fronts at the base, a simple midsection, and an elaborate crown. This time the designers added a

gracefully rounded corner. A good deal of the original embellishment (balconies, cresting, etc.) has been stripped away along with the original corner shop window, but the building is still handsome.

𝟛𝟘 325 Fifth Avenue

2004–6 · STEPHEN JACOBS AND ANDI PEPPER

A 42-story condominium tower bristling with balconies offering views of the Empire State Building.

𝟛𝟙 Hotel Aberdeen

17 West 32nd Street

1902–4 · HARRY B. MULLIKAN

It is easy to imagine that the owner and architect here saw themselves in direct competition with the contemporary Hotel Wolcott and worked to create a building with even more decorative drama. The center of the deeply rusticated lower floors is dominated by a vigorously sculptural entrance portal with a protruding balcony. The real stars are the hard-working Atalantes heroically supporting an improbable load of masonry. Above the entry, a projecting bay of windows with decorative spandrels leads the eye upward to a broken pediment at the tenth story.

❷ Empire State Building

350 Fifth Avenue

1929–31 · SHREVE, LAMB & HARMON

This is, of course, one of New York's most recognizable buildings—a symbol, almost a trademark, of the city. For nearly forty years it was also the world's tallest structure. The Empire State Building has lost that distinction, but it is still a splendid building with a great story.

In 1927 a group of investors led by General Motors and DuPont executive John J. Raskob acquired the site of the Waldorf-Astoria and adjacent properties in order to erect a speculative office building. Raskob recruited former New York State Governor Al Smith to be the public face of the project, and William Lamb was engaged as the designer. As plans developed, Raskob became determined to build the world's tallest building, surpassing the Chrysler Building and 40 Wall Street then under construction.

The program included only a short list of requirements: the building had to be erected on a strict budget, the distance between a window and any internal workspace could be no more than 28 feet, and there should be as many stories as financially feasible. The developers also specified limestone as the cladding and required that construction be completed by May 1, 1931. The design evolved directly from these strictures as well as zoning regulations, elevator requirements, and budget exigencies. This was, after all, not a vanity or image building like the Chrysler or Woolworth Buildings, but a speculative project that needed to pay its own way. Final plans called for 86 stories, topped by a 14-story mast, bringing the structure's total height to 1,250 feet.

Lamb's design is brilliant, stressing simplicity of detail, long unbroken visual lines, and beautiful modern materials. The facade is organized around paired vertical strips of aluminum windows and spandrels, projecting slightly from the limestone wall. Window strips and stonework were simplified as much as possible to permit off-

site fabrication and efficient installation. The building's style emerged naturally from economic and technical choices. The Empire State is neither flamboyant nor art deco in the usual sense. It is simply modern.

The start of construction in October 1929 coincided almost exactly with the stock market crash. Raskob was determined to press ahead and the contractors, Starrett Brothers, did not let him down. Thanks to brilliant organization, careful prefabrication of components, and a furious work pace of close to four and a half floors per week, the Empire State Building was erected in an astonishing eighteen months. It opened ahead of schedule and under budget. This was fortunate since tenants were scarce in early years. Only in the 1950s did the building begin to break even.

A recent restoration has highlighted the clean, elegant, understated design, and the careful use of color and materials. At street level the five-story base, which fills the entire site, dominates. Zoning rules would have allowed this base to be 12 stories tall before mandatory set-back requirements kicked in, but Lamb chose to keep it low to minimize the mass of the building at street level and to permit the tower to rise cleanly and symmetrically from the base.

The main lobby facing Fifth Avenue is appropriately spectacular. Three stories tall, it is adorned with multi-colored marble, bronze medallions, and patterned golden ceiling. A portrait of the building radiating electronic programming across the region closes the vista. The entrance to the perennially popular observation deck is on 34th Street.

㉝ B. Altman and Company Building

355–371 Fifth Avenue

1905–13 · TROWBRIDGE & LIVINGSTON; FACADE SIMPLIFIED IN 1936;
EXTERIOR RESTORED BY HARDY HOLZMAN PFEIFFER AND INTERIOR
CONVERSION BY GWATHMEY SIEGEL ASSOCIATES, 1996

Benjamin Altman began his
business in a small shop on Third
Avenue at 9th Street. In 1874
he relocated to Sixth Avenue at
19th Street on the Ladies' Mile.
His decision twenty-five years
later to move to Fifth Avenue
was a calculated gamble. The
new location placed him on a
prominent corner of fashionable street on the edge of the conservative
and wealthy Murray Hill neighborhood and almost equidistant
from Pennsylvania Station and Grand Central Terminal, both under
construction and destined to bring crowds of suburban shoppers into
Manhattan.

Trowbridge & Livingston designed a dignified and understated Italian
palazzo. The classical detailing is bold, but never fussy, the proportions
are excellent. The store was erected in three stages, beginning with
the central section facing 34th Street. The northern part of the Fifth
Avenue facade came next, but the refusal of art dealer Roland Knoedler
to sell his building at the corner of 34th Street delayed the building's
completion. Once the key property had been acquired, the two facades
were seamlessly stitched together. The style remained uniform
throughout, with the exception of the final section facing Madison
Avenue. This wing is not only taller, but it is executed in brick.

Benjamin Altman died in 1913, leaving his remarkable art collection
to the Metropolitan Museum of Art. His store continued in business until
1989. In 1996 the building was adapted for use by the CUNY graduate
school and the New York Public Library.

Across the street on the northwest corner of Fifth Avenue and 34th
Street are the remains of McKim, Mead & White's **Knickerbocker Trust
Building.** ㉞ Stanford White's original design from 1903, built on the
site of A. T. Stewart's mansion, was a sumptuous and refined three-story
Corinthian temple in white marble. Ten stories, also by McKim, Mead &

White, were added in 1921. They remain visible today above a dreary recladding that completely hides the remains of the original temple base.

㉟ Gorham Building

390 Fifth Avenue

1904–6 · STANFORD WHITE OF MCKIM, MEAD & WHITE

The Gorham Manufacturing Company was another Fifth Avenue retail pioneer. This well-known firm of Rhode Island-based silversmiths had maintained a Manhattan showroom since 1859. Gorham occupied a building on Broadway and 19th Street before relocating to Fifth Avenue. Stanford White produced a fine Florentine palazzo for Gorham, complete with a two-story arcade and a crowning loggia. A powerful projecting cornice extends eight feet from the building. It was originally gilded and polychromed. White also designed the delicate bronze frieze just below the cornice over the lower arcade as well as the elegant bronze balcony at the fifth floor complete with twin Gs—fabricated by the Gorham firm itself. The sixth-floor cartouche is by Andrew O'Connor. Gorham moved out in 1923. In subsequent years, the lower floors facing Fifth Avenue were sadly disfigured. The original elevations, although stripped of their sculptural embellishment, are intact along 36th Street.

㊱ Haviland Building

11 East 36th Street

1906–12 · PILCHER & JACHAN

In contrast to the stone palazzi that high-end retailers like Gorham and Altman were erecting on Fifth Avenue, the French porcelain makers

Haviland and Co. chose a more sober and industrial style for their headquarters in Midtown. Haviland filled the first four floors with their merchandise and rented the upper stories of their Tuscan brick and sandstone building with its arcaded bell tower to other tenants. Today, the upper floors, stripped of their original balconies, are apartments.

③⑦ The Langham

400 Fifth Avenue

2010 · GWATHMEY SIEGEL KAUFMAN & ASSOCIATES

This 57-story hotel and apartment tower rises to an illuminated crown that carries on a spirited conversation with the spire of the Empire State Building. The ten-story base was thoughtfully designed to complement the Tiffany, Gorham, and Stewart buildings. The angled windowpanes add welcome texture and depth to the facade.

③⑧ Tiffany & Co. Building

401 Fifth Avenue

1903–6 · STANFORD WHITE OF MCKIM, MEAD & WHITE; RESTORED 2002, BEYER BLINDER BELLE

Here is Stanford White at his peak, designing again for a high-end retailer. Instead of looking to the palaces of Renaissance Florence or Rome for inspiration, White turned to Venice's Grand Canal and specifically to the Palazzo Grimani. To accommodate Tiffany's

showrooms, offices, and workshops White needed a full seven stories, but he grouped the floors into three bands separated by solid cornices and screened by arcades. As was his practice, the architect simplified the original Venetian detailing to accommodate the more enclosed New York setting.

The building originally stood on a low plinth, raising it above the level of the street and setting it apart from its surroundings. The plinth was eliminated when the sidewalk was raised. If the lower half of the pilasters along Fifth Avenue look a bit different from the rest of the building, it is because they are replacements, added during restoration in 2002. The marble is from the original quarry, but it has aged differently.

39 Stewart & Company Building

404 Fifth Avenue
1914 · WARREN & WETMORE

The Stewart Building's eight-story facade is nearly all glass, arranged as so-called "Chicago windows"— tripartite openings with a large fixed central pane flanked by two narrower double-hung windows. Narrow colonettes subdivide the window units. Those areas not given over to glass are faced with handsome blue-and-white terra-cotta panels supplied by the New York Terra-Cotta Company. Their color and style were almost certainly inspired by the eighteenth-century work of Josiah Wedgwood and Robert Adam. Note the beautiful rosettes and the elegant laurel wreaths, ribbons, and bundled reeds. All of this is supported by a steel skeleton erected by the George A. Fuller Company, whose headquarters was the Flatiron Building. Stewart & Co., a women's apparel company, originally occupied half the ground floor while Mark Cross took the other half, relocating north from Madison Square.

40 411 Fifth Avenue

1915 · WARREN & WETMORE

Terra-cotta and stucco everywhere. Above the modern facade at ground

level are wonderful Italian mannerist pilasters, columns, and window surrounds and the Spanish baroque stucco swags at the crown. Over the years the building has housed clothing stores, phonograph retailers, the Red Cross, and the American Commission for Irish Freedom. RCA broadcast the world's first television images from studios here.

④ 420 Fifth Avenue

1989 · BRENNAN BEER GORMAN ARCHITECTS

This 30-story condominium office tower was among the first to offer this form of ownership to business clients. Today it is the home of the Rockefeller Foundation and the Girl Scouts of America.

④ 425 Fifth Avenue

2002 · MICHAEL GRAVES & ASSOCIATES

This sleek 55-story residential tower stands out by virtue of its striking yellow, blue, and white color scheme and the insistent verticality of its detailing. Graves adds additional interest by varying the treatment of the tower's corners: chamfered at the base and crown, cantilevered in between.

⑬ Lord & Taylor Building

424–434 Fifth Avenue
1913–14 · STARRETT & VAN VLECK; OFFICE CONVERSION 2020, BJARKE INGELS GROUP

English merchants Samuel Lord and George Washington Taylor opened their first New York store on Catherine Street in 1826. Business was good, and the firm moved steadily northward—to Grand and Chrystie Streets 1854; Broadway and Grand in 1859; and in 1870 to Broadway and 20th Street on the Ladies' Mile. In 1914 Lord & Taylor opened on Fifth Avenue, continuing in business for more than a century before closing in 2019. The building is currently being converted for office use by its new owner, Amazon.

Compared to other stores in the neighborhood based on Italian palazzo models, Lord & Taylor's brick building is modest. But the design is enlivened by some distinctive features: a prominent chamfered corner, a strong copper cornice, double-height portal, and the large display windows at street level. Above the second floor the windows are detailed with small panes, giving them an appealingly domestic aspect. The handling of the materials, light brick and limestone, is subtly balanced and applied ornament is kept to a minimum. Particularly when viewed from the southeast, the building is poised and dignified. The store's distinctive script logo, created by company president Dorothy Shaver, is painted high on the north wall.

Impressive show windows (particularly during the Christmas holidays) were long a Lord & Taylor specialty. The display windows were designed so that they could be lowered intact to the basement on tracks. Once renewed, they were raised back into position.

⑭ Hardman Piano Building

433 Fifth Avenue
1911 · HARRY ALLAN JACOB

⑮ Knabe Building

437 Fifth Avenue
1904 · C. P. H. GILBERT

This block was long popular with piano manufacturers. The Hardman Building is an elegant white marble palazzo with interiors designed to evoke those of a private mansion. Two doors to the north, competitor Knabe favored a classic Beaux-Arts composition culminating in a tall dormered mansard. This crowning level was all for show; the mansard is, in fact, only a screen. Knabe moved to a new home at 657 Fifth Avenue in 1928, at which time the ground floor received its present awkward treatment.

46 Farmer's Loan & Trust Building

435 Fifth Avenue

1906 · EDWIN WILBUR; EXPANDED 1911, ROBERT TELCHMAN

Farmer's Loan & Trust was designed to look like a standard loft building rather than an august financial institution. But this may have been the plan from the start. The bank soon moved north to 475 Fifth Avenue, retaining 435 as a rental property. A mansard was added in 1911 to provide additional space.

❹ Stavros Niarchos Foundation Library
(Arnold Constable Building)

455 Fifth Avenue

1914 · JAMES T. BARTLEY;
RENOVATED 2018–20, MECANOO
AND BEYER BLINDER BELLE

The current home of the New York Public Library's Midtown branch was built for Arnold Constable & Company. When it closed in 1975, it was New York's oldest department store. The library moved in shortly thereafter. A major renovation supported by the Niarchos Foundation has transformed what was for forty years a dismal dungeon into a clean, open, light-filled space for books and people. The upper floors are organized around a central atrium ringed with book stacks. At the top, the roof offers an open-air terrace with great views and a café. There is space for 400,000 volumes, including circulating collections, a business library, and a dedicated children's area.

❹ 461 Fifth Avenue

1988 · SKIDMORE, OWINGS & MERRILL

If the Niarchos Library breathes the dignified spirt of Fifth Avenue past, its neighbor across 40th Street reflects the preferences of a very different era. The 10-story base, despite some fussy detailing, respects the materials and roof line of its neighbors. The 18-story set-back tower, on the other hand, is an anthology of once fashionable postmodern motifs like the abstracted pediments applied at intervals to the facade.

④⑨ Knox Building
(HSBC)

452 Fifth Avenue
1901–2 · JOHN DUNCAN; 1964, KAHN
& JACOBS; 1981–83, ATTIA & PERKINS;
RESTORED 2010, PBDW ARCHITECTS

In earlier times, no respectable man would be seen in public without a proper hat, and for years the Knox Hat Company was the supplier of choice. The firm's Fifth Avenue home is a classic Beaux-Arts composition in brick and stone: a rusticated facade, large scale ornamental details, and mansard roof. The seventh-floor balcony and the finally detailed dormer with its torch and anthemia cresting, and eagles are particularly lush. The architect has skillfully exploited the prominent corner site facing what would be New York's new public library.

The survival of Duncan's building is a great preservation success. In 1964 the Knox Building was acquired by Republic National Bank. In the 1980s Republic (now HSBC) gracefully incorporated it into its New York headquarters, ensuring that the older building retained much of its integrity. 452 Fifth Avenue itself was carefully restored in 2010.

⑤⓪ Farmer's Loan & Trust Building

475 Fifth Avenue
1925–26 · STARRETT & VAN VLECK

During the 1920s business was clearly booming for the Farmer's Loan & Trust. This building is quite a step up from their modest former home at 435 Fifth Avenue. A charming frieze of terra-cotta panels with peacocks and foxes rings the building above the first floor. Marble panels enrich the spandrels at the next level, and projecting gargoyles glower down at us from the rooftop.

⬦→ 40th Street

40th Street runs along the southern edge of Bryant Park. The park was created 1847 to fill the western half of the block behind the Croton Reservoir. This was the site in 1853 of New York's first world's fair, *The Exhibition of the Industry of All Nations*. In 1884 the park was renamed for journalist William Cullen Bryant. By the 1980s Bryant Park was a derelict and dangerous place. Thanks to restoration by Hanna/Olin and Hardy Holzman Pfeiffer completed in 1982, Bryant Park is now one of the city's liveliest oases. Underneath are the relocated book stacks of the library. At the east end is a handsome memorial to the park's namesake. The statue is by Herbert Adams, the setting by Carrère and Hastings.

🅐 The Bryant

16 West 40th Street

2013–17 · DAVID CHIPPERFIELD

This is the British architect's first ground-up project in Manhattan, a hotel and condominium combination of understated elegance. The building rises as a traditional freestanding tower from a five-story base. The first 16 floors are occupied by a hotel; apartments fill the remaining levels. Here broad sliding windows open onto shallow balconies behind a grid of soft white concrete panels. The materials and elevation are carefully considered to ensure that it is a good neighbor on this historic block.

🅑 Engineers' Club

32 West 40th Street

1905–7 · WHITFIELD & KING

The Engineers' Club was founded in 1888. In 1904 Andrew Carnegie, a member, paid for this new clubhouse, designed by Henry Whitfield,

his brother-in-law. Carnegie also supported the construction of a separate but connected building on 39th Street to house several related engineering societies. The main 12-story Renaissance revival building with its top-floor loggia included not only social spaces but also 66 bedrooms that served as bachelor apartments for young engineers. Today the building houses cooperative apartments.

ⓒ American Radiator Building
Bryant Park Hotel

40 West 40th Street
1923–24 · RAYMOND HOOD;
HOTEL CONVERSION 2001,
DAVID CHIPPERFIELD

This is one of New York's most distinctive and arresting skyscrapers, the work of Raymond Hood, who also designed the Daily News and McGraw Hill Buildings, and who was influential in the planning of Rockefeller Center. American Radiator is not just a stylish addition to the skyline, but also an effective corporate trademark. The lower floors are faced with highly polished granite and pierced with two-story show windows to either side of a central portal embellished with Gothic detailing. At the third level, a detailed cornice is supported by spirited medieval corbels.

Higher up, the Middle Ages give way to a series of golden pinnacles and spandrels. The dark brick shaft rises as a freestanding tower through a series of powerful cubic setbacks and additional pinnacles to a complex golden crown— the apotheosis of the radiator. It's an amazing performance, particularly at night when dramatically floodlit.

🗴 Astor Trust Building

501 Fifth Avenue

1915–16 · ERNEST FLAGG;
RESTORATION 2013, BOHLIN
CYWINSKI JACKSON

Sober and dignified as befits a
bank founded by one of New
York's oldest real estate families.

Flagg worked to ensure that his building was a respectful neighbor to the
recently completed New York Public Library across the street.

🗴 New York Public Library

Stephen A. Schwarzman Building

476 Fifth Avenue

1898–1911 · CARRÈRE & HASTINGS

Set back from the street and raised on a block-long terrace, the Carrère
& Hastings building presides with grace and serene confidence over the
important intersection of Fifth Avenue and 42nd Street.

The New York Public Library was formed in 1895 through the consoli-
dation of three private organizations: the Astor Library, the Lenox Library,
and the Tilden Trust. In 1901 the New York Free Circulating Library,
sponsored by Andrew Carnegie, was also incorporated. The resulting
institution aspired to become one of the world's greatest libraries, and it
needed an appropriately grand home.

Following the removal of the Croton Reservoir in 1890, a competition
for the prestigious library commission was held, and Carrère & Hastings

bested a number of larger and better-known firms. The symmetrical, classical design, developed from a tightly defined functional program drawn up by the Library Director John S. Billings, owes much to the principles of the École des Beaux-Arts where both designers had studied.

The triumphal arch entry is adorned with figures by Paul Wayland Bartlett representing the different areas of knowledge available for study inside: History, Romance, Religion, Poetry, Drama, Philosophy. The fountains in the niches to either side contain personifications of Truth and Beauty. At the extreme south and north ends of the facade are pediments by George Grey Barnard depicting Art and History.

Climbing the broad steps past Edward Potter's regal lions (named Patience and Fortitude by Mayor Fiorello LaGuardia) and passing through the entry arches, visitors arrive in august but welcoming vaulted marble lobby. To either side, grand staircases lead up two flights to an impressive rotunda with mural paintings, *The Story of the Recorded Word*, executed under the WPA by Edward Laning. From there the reader's processional route leads through the catalog room to the magnificent main reading room. Brilliantly lit by large windows, it sits atop ten floors of bookstacks, high above the noise and bustle of the city. The room, 297 feet long and 78 feet wide, offers a full half acre of column free space separated into two parts by a central vestibule and book delivery station. The loosely Italian Renaissance design is warm, lush, and deeply serious. Every detail from the sumptuous Venetian ceiling to the bookshelves, reading desk lamps, overhead chandeliers, and even the door handles were specially designed for the space. The room reopened after a careful and respectful restoration in 2016.

On the way back down to street level, take note of the beautiful detailing of the hallways and staircases and of the statues of the two architects in niches at the bottom of the stairs in the entry hall. They deserve the recognition.

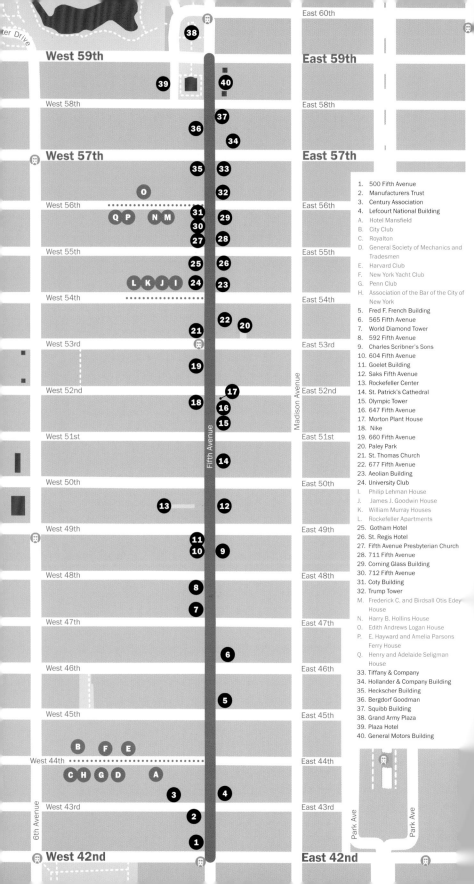

West 59th · East 59th
East 60th
West 58th · East 58th
West 57th · East 57th
West 56th · East 56th
West 55th · East 55th
West 54th · East 54th
West 53rd · East 53rd
West 52nd · East 52nd
West 51st · East 51st
West 50th · East 50th
West 49th · East 49th
West 48th · East 48th
West 47th · East 47th
West 46th · East 46th
West 45th · East 45th
West 44th · East 44th
West 43rd · East 43rd
West 42nd · East 42nd

Fifth Avenue
Madison Avenue
Park Ave
6th Avenue

1. 500 Fifth Avenue
2. Manufacturers Trust
3. Century Association
4. Lefcourt National Building
A. Hotel Mansfield
B. City Club
C. Royalton
D. General Society of Mechanics and Tradesmen
E. Harvard Club
F. New York Yacht Club
G. Penn Club
H. Association of the Bar of the City of New York
5. Fred F. French Building
6. 565 Fifth Avenue
7. World Diamond Tower
8. 592 Fifth Avenue
9. Charles Scribner's Sons
10. 604 Fifth Avenue
11. Goelet Building
12. Saks Fifth Avenue
13. Rockefeller Center
14. St. Patrick's Cathedral
15. Olympic Tower
16. 647 Fifth Avenue
17. Morton Plant House
18. Nike
19. 660 Fifth Avenue
20. Paley Park
21. St. Thomas Church
22. 677 Fifth Avenue
23. Aeolian Building
24. University Club
I. Philip Lehman House
J. James J. Goodwin House
K. William Murray Houses
L. Rockefeller Apartments
25. Gotham Hotel
26. St. Regis Hotel
27. Fifth Avenue Presbyterian Church
28. 711 Fifth Avenue
29. Corning Glass Building
30. 712 Fifth Avenue
31. Coty Building
32. Trump Tower
M. Frederick C. and Birdsall Otis Edey House
N. Harry B. Hollins House
O. Edith Andrews Logan House
P. E. Hayward and Amelia Parsons Ferry House
Q. Henry and Adelaide Seligman House
33. Tiffany & Company
34. Hollander & Company Building
35. Heckscher Building
36. Bergdorf Goodman
37. Squibb Building
38. Grand Army Plaza
39. Plaza Hotel
40. General Motors Building

CHAPTER 3

New York Public Library to Grand Army Plaza

When they were first developed during the middle years of the nineteenth century, the blocks of Fifth Avenue between the Croton Reservoir and Central Park were dotted with asylums, hospitals, and schools. A cattle farm operated nearby until the 1860s. The area changed dramatically following the Civil War when these institutions were replaced by mansions, clubs, and houses of worship.

For about forty years beginning in the 1880s, Fifth Avenue in the upper 50s was home to New York's most spectacular dwellings. To a very significant degree, this was Vanderbilt country. The family spent millions buying up real estate and then set about erecting a group of eight increasingly elaborate mansions between 51st and 59th Streets. Other wealthy families followed, and at the turn of the twentieth century, the corner of Fifth Avenue and 57th Street was *the* location at which to build a mansion, Collis and Arabella Huntington's imposing house filled the southeast corner. William C. Whitney's somber red-brick mansion occupied the southwest corner. Diagonally opposite sat Mary Mason Jones's lavishly Parisian home, part of what was known as "Marble Row." Grandest of all was the French chateau that George B. Post designed for Cornelius Vanderbilt II on the northwest corner.

As the wealthy settled in the neighborhood, established Protestant congregations began to build handsome new churches in Midtown. They were followed in short order by other denominations that elected to build along Fifth Avenue to assert their growing confidence and influence. By the mid-1880s, there were seven major houses of worship along Fifth Avenue between 43rd and 56th Streets. Today only St. Patrick's, St. Thomas, and Fifth Avenue Presbyterian remain.

Shortly after the turn of the twentieth century, the completion of Grand Central Terminal transformed the character of Fifth Avenue and 42nd Street. With easy railway access to Midtown from the suburbs for shoppers and commuters, the blocks within the orbit of the terminal first became prime retail territory and subsequently one of Manhattan's leading business districts. For many years, the corner of Fifth Avenue and 42nd Street was regarded as one of New York's most desirable and expensive business addresses, rivaling the intersection of Broadway and Wall Street. The recent completion of One Vanderbilt, a 93-story glass and terra-cotta office tower (2017–20; Kohn Pedersen Fox) adjacent to Grand Central, is testimony to the continuing power of the terminal to shape the development of the blocks nearby.

The construction of Rockefeller Center from 1931 to 1939 on the west side of Fifth Avenue between 48th and 51st Streets was equally transformational. Blocks of aging brownstones were swept away. In their place arose a glamorous new center for business, shopping, dining, and entertainment. In the years that followed, Fifth Avenue in the upper 50s emerged as the center for high-end retail and luxury hotels, including the St. Regis and the Plaza, Cartier, Tiffany's, and Bergdorf Goodman as well as flagships for European brands like Armani, Bulgari, Ferragamo, and Louis Vuitton. This stretch of Fifth Avenue ends at Grand Army Plaza, one of Manhattan's great public spaces and a fitting introduction to Central Park.

❶ 500 Fifth Avenue

1929–31 · SHREVE, LAMB & HARMON

Designed by the architects of the Empire State Building, 500 Fifth Avenue is, in its way, an equally notable contribution to the New York skyline. This was an expensive site and developer Walter Salmon needed every inch of rentable space allowed under the 1916 zoning rules. Even more complicated, sections of the parcel he assembled were in two zoning districts with different setback requirements. William Lamb worked creatively within these strictures to create a wonderful abstract composition.

As at the Empire State Building, the upper floors at 500 Fifth are virtually unornamented. The main expressive feature of the tower is the almost uninterrupted vertical line of windows at the center of each facade. They draw the eye skyward through 59 stories of carefully laid brick to the terra-cotta chevrons of the crown. At ground level, there are understated art deco motifs carved into the limestone, light-green metal spandrels, and a limestone and black-granite entry portal on Fifth Avenue. The gilded relief over the door by Edmond Armateis is titled *The Genius of the Modern Skyscraper*.

❷ Manufacturers Trust

510 Fifth Avenue

1953–54 · GORDON BUNSHAFT OF SKIDMORE, OWINGS & MERRILL

Although the banking business in America had grown dramatically in size and complexity during the first half of the twentieth century, bank buildings were often still conservatively and stolidly designed. Manufacturers Trust sought to convey something quite different. Founded as a neighborhood bank, the company worked hard to project friendliness and accessibility, promoting customer service as well as financial security. In commissioning this new and highly visible Fifth Avenue branch, the management specifically asked SOM and Bunshaft to design a building that was modern, open, and inviting.

The result is a transparent box inspired by the work of Mies van der Rohe and his associates. Curtain walls of clear glass (the largest panes ever used at the time) rise from a low black-granite plinth. The glass wall is supported and delineated by a framework of aluminum mullions and rails interspersed with dark-gray spandrel panels that conceal the floor slabs. Originally there was no entrance on Fifth Avenue, but the building's identity was clearly and dramatically advertised by the presence of the enormous 30-ton vault door (designed by Henry Dreyfuss) just behind the clear glass wall.

Inside, the cantilevered upper banking floor seems to float free of the non-structural walls. Here architecture meant not solid walls but transparent planes delineating a volume. Today the bank is gone, replaced by a clothing store. Many interior changes have been made, but a 70-foot paneled metal screen by artist Harry Bertoia, removed in 2010, has been returned to this spare and refined building after a successful preservation battle.

The vacant lot at the northwest corner of Fifth Avenue and 43rd Street is slated to become the site of Fifth Avenue's second tallest building: a 70-story mixed-use tower (520 Fifth Avenue) designed by Kohn Pedersen

Fox. The building's great height was made possible by the transfer of air rights from several landmarked buildings in the area, including the Century Association.

❸ Century Association

7 West 43rd Street

1889–91 · STANFORD WHITE OF MCKIM, MEAD & WHITE

This is the second home of a distinguished club founded in 1847 to "promote the advancement of art and literature." The architects provided members with an elegant Renaissance palace (based on the Palazzo Canossa in Verona), symmetrical, balanced, and sumptuously decorated.

The base is stone, but everything above is brick and terra-cotta, embellished by White with a rich variety of patterns, textures, and flourishes. It's a virtuoso performance with the possibility of decorative excess held in check by fine proportions and careful symmetry, centered on the arched entry portal and the beautiful Palladian window above.

❹ Lefcourt National Building

521 Fifth Avenue

1929 · SHREVE, LAMB & HARMON

Another carefully massed composition by Shreve, Lamb & Harmon. Here the developer was A. E. Lefcourt who started his working life with a pushcart on the Lower East Side and went on to develop many of the loft buildings in the garment district.

⬦ 44th Street

The **Hotel Mansfield** Ⓐ (12 West 44th Street; 1901–2; Renwick, Aspinwall & Owen) is a striking stone and brick Beaux-Arts apartment hotel that catered, like many in the neighborhood, to well-off bachelors eager to live in this fashionable part of town. The three stacks of copper-clad oriel windows and the crowning mansard are particularly appealing.

There are a number of similar hotels farther along the block, all built around the same time: the Iroquois (49 West 44th Street; 1903; Harry B. Mulliken), the **City Club** Ⓑ (55 West 44th Street; 1901–4; Lord & Hewlett) originally built to house the club of that name, and the **Royalton** Ⓒ (44 West 44th Street; 1898; Rossiter & Wright) with its imposing pedimented entry. In 1988 the Royalton's interior was redesigned in high style by Philippe Starck. At the end of the block is the celebrated Algonquin (59 West 44th Street; 1902; Goldwin Starrett). All are worth a look as variations on a theme.

Between the bookends of the Mansfield and the Algonquin are other architectural treasures.

D General Society of Mechanics and Tradesmen

20 West 44th Street

1891 · LAMB & RICH; EXTENDED
1909, RALPH S. TOWNSEND

The Society, founded in 1785, continues to provide free professional development classes for workers in the trades and skilled crafts. The Society has a fine library, offers a public lecture program, and is the home of a truly remarkable collection of historic locks and keys. There is a copy of the Parthenon frieze above the ionic columns at the center of the facade and elegantly embellished fire escapes to either side.

E Harvard Club

27 West 44th Street

1893–94 WITH LATER ADDITIONS · CHARLES MCKIM OF MCKIM, MEAD & WHITE; 2003 ADDITION, MAX BOND OF DAVIS BRODY BOND

Exuding poise and confidence, the Harvard Club is a solid but elegant composition in brick and limestone that alludes to the Federal-style gates of Harvard Yard, also designed by McKim. Throughout, the architectural components are bold and sculptural, the detailing careful and refined. Later additions, also by McKim, Mead & White, extended the original structure to the west and through the block to 45th Street. The latest addition, by Max Bond, is a foil to the original architecture.

F New York Yacht Club

37 West 44th Street

1899–1900 · WARREN & WETMORE

Understated is not the first word that comes to mind to describe this splendid clubhouse, long home to the America's Cup trophy. The basic style is Beaux-Arts but inflected everywhere with nautical motifs. Warren

was himself a yachtsman and drew on his personal collection of ship drawings for inspiration. The voluptuous windows into the library are designed to recall the sterns of galleons. Below are seaweed garlands and dolphins spewing water. The asymmetrically placed entrance is surmounted by a splendid cartouche and is flanked higher up on the wall by twin flagstaffs and the club's crests. Several floors up, a pergola crowns a building that a period critic described as "ostentatious but ingenious." This was Whitney Warren's first major commission, and he made the most of it.

G Penn Club

30 West 44th Street
1900–1901 · TRACY & SWARTWOUT

Originally intended for Yale University graduates, this was one of the first high-rise clubs in the city. Yale relocated in 1915, and there have been several tenants over the years with the University of Pennsylvania now in residence. The most dramatic architectural feature of this classic Beaux-Arts design is the boldly projecting and bracketed copper cornice.

H Association of the Bar of the City of New York

42 West 44th Street
1895–96 · CYRUS L. W. EIDLITZ

One enters through a recessed porch marked by two austere fluted Doric columns. Above, the facade is a carefully organized composition of classical friezes, cornices, and Corinthian pilasters punctuated by simple window openings. This is a strong, somewhat severe building with considerable presence and real personality.

❺ Fred F. French Building

551 Fifth Avenue
1926–27 · H. DOUGLAS IVES WITH SLOAN & ROBERTSON

Fred French was one of the most active real estate developers in New York during the late 1920 and early 1930s. This building was his corporate headquarters.

Most of the great skyscrapers erected during the 1920s were slim, freestanding towers. Such buildings are great skyline landmarks and can be potent corporate symbols, but they present distinct economic challenges. As a tower rises, mandated setbacks reduce the size of the rentable floorplates. Developers like French sought creative ways to exploit zoning regulations to create tall, eye-catching buildings that would also generate a satisfactory return on investment.

This site straddled several differently zoned land parcels. Douglas Ives responded to the challenge with a ziggurat-like base that rises through multiple setbacks to support a flat slab, a strategy that became a model for Sloan & Robertson's Chanin Building on 42nd Street and Lexington Avenue and the RCA Building in Rockefeller Center.

The architects embellished the building with Mesopotamian motifs, making lavish use of enameled brick and terra-cotta. The decoration becomes more elaborate as the building rises, culminating in a remarkable ceramic relief at the top of the tower emblazoned with a rising sun. At the ground level, and particularly around the two gilded entry portals, the Near Eastern theme is enriched with stylized Egyptian and classical motifs. The main lobby is splendid: polychromed vaults, gilt bronze elevator doors, a wealth of marble, eight architect-designed bronze and glass chandeliers, and one of the great letter boxes in New York.

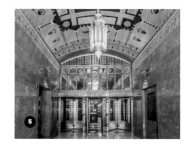

⑥ 565 Fifth Avenue

1993 · NORMAN JAFFE

A beautifully crisp and carefully detailed update of such classic International Style buildings as Manufacturers Trust. Glass, steel, and concrete are combined with great finesse. The lower floors are currently sheathed in decorative metal trusswork, but the view of the upper floors is unimpeded. The coolly impressive and tightly designed lobby in gridded steel and gray marble is around the corner on 46th Street behind a dramatic entrance canopy.

47th Street to the west of Fifth Avenue is "Diamond District Way." Marked by triumphant gem-themed gateway lamp standards. 580 Fifth Avenue, the **World Diamond Tower** ❼ (1925; Warren & Wetmore) offers some crisp Gothic and heraldic decoration, particularly at the crown.

⑧ 592 Fifth Avenue

1964 · HAUSMAN & ROSENBERG; 2018, YSHIHARA MCKEE

592 Fifth Avenue has sustained some dramatic changes over the years. The building began life in 1911 as a dignified French classical design by Carrère & Hastings for the jewelers Black, Starr & Frost. In 1964 Hausman & Rosenberg reclad the facade in marble for Bank of America with peculiar lozenge-shaped windows. Most recently Yshihara Mckee applied a trendy geometrically delineated update but retained the 1964 window pattern.

❾ Charles Scribner's Sons

597 Fifth Avenue

1912–13 · ERNEST FLAGG

Scribner's first Fifth Avenue headquarters was downtown at 22nd Street. This is the publisher's subsequent home, designed by the same architect (Scribner's brother-in-law) and located at what by 1912 had become a more fashionable address. The two buildings are clear cousins, but the uptown structure is larger and more richly detailed. Flagg provided Scribner's with a building of elegance and sophistication, fully worthy of Hemingway, Fitzgerald, Ring Lardner, and Thomas Wolfe whose works were published here.

The most immediately striking feature is the two-story iron and glass show window that opens into the grand vaulted and balconied interior, a versatile space that once housed Scribner's book shop and is now home to a clothing store. The black metal screen, carefully preserved, features a graceful central elliptical arch, set off with sinuous art nouveau detailing in gold.

At the fourth level is a richly decorated stone balcony accented with portrait medallions of great printers of the past: Benjamin Franklin, William Caxton, Johannes Gutenberg, Aldus Manutius. Three bays of dark metal-framed windows dominate the center of the facade. Above the simple cornice is a mansard roof with a central dormer window. Flagg is quoted as saying that good architecture should mimic the human form: "symmetry from left to right, and diversity from head to foot" —a good description of the Scribner Building.

⑩ 604 Fifth Avenue

1924 · WILLIAM VAN ALEN

Built originally for the once-famous Child's Restaurant chain, 604 Fifth was an eye-catching architectural pioneer in 1924—sleek, clean, determinedly modern. Van Alen, who went on to design the Chrysler Building, created what was described as a jewel box: broad panes of plate glass set flush in white limestone. This was among the first buildings in New York to utilize curved glass-block corner windows.

⑪ Goelet Building

608 Fifth Avenue
1930–32 · VICTOR L. S. HAFNER
OF E. H. FAILE & CO.

The Goelet family house stood on this site from 1882 until 1929. With Rockefeller Center about to rise across the street, Robert Goelet seized the opportunity to replace his mansion with a commercial structure. The result is a building that combines sumptuously applied traditional materials with the latest in modern curtain wall technology.

608 Fifth Avenue meets the street with two stories of show windows set off by dark green marble panels. The upper levels are distinctively and luxuriously articulated in two shades of marble, creating a balanced play of the vertical and horizontal elements. Terraces and a recessed penthouse complete the composition. The lobby is an art deco treasure in silver leaf, black marble, and pierced metal.

🄬 Saks Fifth Avenue

611 Fifth Avenue

1922–24 · STARRETT & VAN VLECK

Saks was a late arrival to Fifth Avenue, but this store played a key role in shifting the center of gravity for high-end retailing northward. The Saks building is a variation on the understated, businesslike style which the architects applied to Lord & Taylor. Note the chamfered corners, Italian palazzo detailing (rusticated ground floor, Corinthian pilasters, decorative cornices) and large display windows. The building could not have a better location. When Rockefeller Center opened, Saks was directly on axis with the main promenade.

🄭 Rockefeller Center

1931–39 · ASSOCIATED ARCHITECTS; MANY LATER ADDITIONS AND ALTERATIONS

Rockefeller Center is one of America's great architectural and urbanistic achievements: a unified skyscraper metropolis, a city within the city. With its skating rink, annual Christmas tree, observation deck, broadcasting studios, and the Radio City Music Hall, it is one of New York's great attractions, a gathering place for visitors and residents alike.

Rockefeller Center's story begins in 1927 and involves three key players: Columbia University, which owned twelve acres of land along Fifth Avenue from 48th to 51st Street (the site of its former campus); the Metropolitan Opera, which was eager to build a new theater to replace its outdated home on Broadway; and John D. Rockefeller Jr., who lived just a few blocks north and had money to invest. The plan was for Rockefeller to lease the land from Columbia, make the central plot available to the opera, and then sublease the rest for commercial development. After the stock market crashed, the opera backed out, and Rockefeller was left with an expensive lease for a large parcel of land. He decided to develop the property himself.

The design of the Center was the work of three architectural firms known as the Associated Architects: Reinhard & Hofmeister; Corbett,

Harrison & MacMurray; and Hood & Fouilhoux. While the architectural image is very much of its moment, the overall layout is classic Beaux-Arts—a group of carefully scaled and sequenced buildings arranged along distinct axes and focused on a central plaza. The Center is oriented toward Fifth Avenue where the modestly scaled Maison Française and British Empire buildings flank a central promenade known as the Channel Gardens. The promenade slopes down as it moves west past planting beds, fountains, and flanking stores and terminates in a sunken plaza (a skating rink in winter) anchored by sculptor Paul Manship's gilded figure of Prometheus. Soaring above is the prow of the 70-story RCA Building (30 Rockefeller Plaza), the centerpiece of the complex. Around the plaza are a balanced but asymmetrical group of buildings. A private street mid-block establishes a secondary north–south axis.

All the original buildings are constructed of the same Indiana limestone with understated gray aluminum trim. The complex is further united by an ambitious program of sculptural decoration. In addition to Manship's *Prometheus,* highlights include Lee Lawrie's *Atlas* in front of the International Building on Fifth Avenue and his dynamic relief of *Wisdom* (cribbed from visionary British artist William Blake) over the entrance to the RCA Building. Hildreth Meière provided the spirited enamel plaques on the exterior of Radio City Music Hall. Other buildings have decorative elements relating to their tenants. Isamu Noguchi's powerful stainless-steel relief *News* adorns the former Associated Press Building, and the nationally themed embellishments of the British and French buildings facing Fifth Avenue add stylish grace notes. Radio City Music Hall's glamorous art deco interior is legendary, as are the somber black and gold lobbies of the RCA and International Buildings—symphonies of fine materials, ambitious murals, and carefully executed details.

The Center includes more amenities than can be seen from street level. Nearly all the original buildings featured a roof top garden. Underground a vast network of sleek concourses offers shopping and dining as well as access to the subway. Hidden away farther below street level are ramps and docks for deliveries.

⓮ St. Patrick's Cathedral

50th to 51st Street

1858–79 · JAMES RENWICK, JR.; ARCHBISHOP'S RESIDENCE, 1880; SPIRES, 1888; LADY CHAPEL, 1906, CHARLES T. MATHEWS; RESTORATION 2012–15, MURPHY BURNHAM & BUTTRICK

In the mid-nineteenth century, due largely to Irish and Italian immigration, New York's Roman Catholic population exploded. This limestone cathedral is a powerful testament to that community's increasing size and influence. The building, which replaced St. Patrick's Old Cathedral on Mulberry Street as the seat of the Archdiocese of New York, was in every sense a statement.

James Renwick, who up to this point had worked only on parish churches for Protestant clients, drew freely on English, French, and particularly German models for his design. He did his research well and skillfully combined a full lexicon of Gothic features. St. Patrick's has it all: an impressive west front with a triple portal executed in marble, two 330-foot spires, and a central rose window, all elaborately detailed. The north and south transepts with their crockets and pinnacles are only slightly less richly ornamented than the main entrance. Inside, the long nave, aisles, ambulatory, and transepts are fully vaulted (albeit in plaster) and every window is richly glazed. The overall effect is impressive, if somewhat cool and academic. There is more architectural energy in the Lady Chapel (added in 1906) behind the High Altar. The inlaid marble altar frontal (1941) is by Hildreth Meière.

⑮ Olympic Tower

645 Fifth Avenue

1976 · SKIDMORE, OWINGS & MERRILL

Built by Aristotle Onassis on the site of the Best & Company clothing store, Olympic Tower rises sheer, dark, and somewhat oppressively from the street line. This is among the first New York buildings to combine offices, condominiums, and retail in a single structure. Residences are up top, and there is a recently renovated public passage, complete with panels of "green wall," running from 51st to 52nd Streets.

⑯ 647 Fifth Avenue

1902–5 · HUNT & HUNT

In 1900 this stretch of Fifth Avenue was lined with mansions belonging to the Vanderbilt family. This house is the only survivor. It was originally one of a pair known as the "Marble Twins" commissioned by George

Washington Vanderbilt, grandson of the Commodore. Vanderbilt never lived in either of the houses. He chose instead to settle in his "chateau," Biltmore, in North Carolina. If 647 Fifth Avenue looks a bit ungainly today, this is the result of multiple alterations. An additional story was grafted on top in 1917 and a low stoop and English basement were removed when the building was converted for retail use. In later years 647 Fifth Avenue housed the art dealers Wildenstein & Co. and is now Versace's New York flagship store.

⓱ Morton Plant House
(Cartier)

651 Fifth Avenue

1903–5 · ROBERT W. GIBSON;
CONVERTED FOR RETAIL USE, 1917,
WILLIAM WELLES BOSWORTH;
ADJACENT AND CONNECTED HOUSE
ON 52ND STREET, 1905, C. P. H.
GILBERT

The Morton Plant House is wonderfully intact: a beautiful French classical mansion in granite and marble with elegant detailing. The main entry facade facing 52nd Street is particularly impressive with its shallow central pediment and pilasters under a strong cornice.

Plant secured the land for his house from William K. Vanderbilt, but he was required to pledge that the site would not be converted to commercial use for twenty-five years. By 1917, however, the character of Fifth Avenue was changing, and Plant, with Vanderbilt's permission, sold his house to the jeweler Pierre Cartier. Cartier negotiated an interesting deal: he paid Plant $100 plus a celebrated pearl necklace, coveted by Mrs. Plant, for the building.

⓲ Nike

650 Fifth Avenue

2018 · ROCKWELL GROUP; WITH MODE LAB, CALLISONRTKL,
AND HEINTGES CONSULTING ARCHITECTS & ENGINEERS

Behind a dramatic slumped glass facade Nike's flagship store brands itself the "House of Innovation." There are six floors of dramatic and high-tech showrooms. It is, as Nike claims, "an experience."

⑲ 660 Fifth Avenue

1957 · CARSON & LUNDIN; UPDATED 1999; 2020–22, MAJOR
RENOVATION BY KOHN PEDERSEN FOX

660 Fifth Avenue is the new address for this office building, which is
being renovated and expanded by Kohn Pederson Fox. In its prior
iteration, the building, then known as 666 Fifth Avenue, was notorious for
its textured aluminum facade, considered by many to resemble nothing
so much as a cheese grater. Critics were kinder about the lobby, designed
by Isamu Noguchi and featuring a waterfall, and admired the dramatic
and trendsetting exterior lighting scheme. Stanford White's house for
William K. Vanderbilt II once stood on the site, the successor to the
chateau-like mansion designed for his parents by Richard Morris Hunt.

⑳ Paley Park

3 East 53rd Street

1967 · ZION BREEN RICHARDSON
ASSOCIATES

This is one of New York's earliest,
finest, and most inviting vest-
pocket parks. Just a few steps
off the street is an oasis of calm. Above the granite pavers under foot,
a grove of honey locust trees provides a soft overhead canopy. Ivy
covers the side walls. Straight ahead, filling the entire north wall, is a

20-foot-high waterfall that provides a gentle screen of white noise to drown out the clamor of the city. There are marble tables and wire chairs designed by Harry Bertoia on which to relax. The Park is a POPS (Privately Owned Public Space) donated by former CBS Chairman William S. Paley in honor of his father.

㉑ St. Thomas Church

1 West 53rd Street

1909–14 · CRAM, GOODHUE & FERGUSON

The most striking feature of St. Thomas is its bold asymmetry. Rather than the expected pair of towers, there is only one. But the architects (chiefly Bertram Goodhue) have carefully balanced the simple, powerful mass of that tower against the deep and richly detailed entrance portal and rose window.

The carefully calculated asymmetry continues inside. The wide nave is centered on the entrance portal and is flanked by a pair of very narrow aisles. To the south, tucked behind the tower, is a chapel with its own entrance around the corner. The nave and chancel are beautifully detailed in stone, and everything conspires to direct attention to the carved stone reredos by Lee Lawrie that closes the vista.

Eggers & Higgins, the architects of 680 Fifth Avenue (1957) next door, were careful to design a building that reflects and complements the church. They chose a similarly colored limestone and massed their building to echo the elevation of the church. The two structures play off each other to create a remarkably sympathetic composition.

㉒ 677 Fifth Avenue
(Microsoft)

1930 · W. L. ROUSE & L. A. GOLDSTONE; RENOVATED 2015, GENSLER

The software maker gutted an older building's interior and tacked on a shiny new facade. A reminder of what went before can be seen up top. This was the Cammeyer Building, built in 1930 on the site of yet another Vanderbilt mansion.

㉓ Aeolian Building

689 Fifth Avenue
1925–27 · WARREN & WETMORE

This playfully designed building was originally the home of the Aeolian Company, leading makers of player pianos, organs, and other mechanical musical instruments. The cusped

windows and bronze garlands on the lower floors originally signaled the location of the piano showroom. The midsection is vertically articulated with smooth flat masonry piers and a softly rounded corner. Decoration breaks loose again at the ninth floor with balconies, more swags, multiple setbacks, arched windows, a curved cornice and, at the top, a picturesque little tower with a lantern. Whitney Warren and Charles

Wetmore began their partnership with the New York Yacht Club. Here, at the end of their active careers, they created a similarly lighthearted design.

❷❹ University Club

1 West 54th Street

1897–99 · CHARLES MCKIM OF MCKIM, MEAD & WHITE;
ADDITION TO THE WEST

Charles McKim provided club members with an assured and stately Italian palazzo in pink granite, inspired chiefly by fifteenth-century Florentine models. McKim had to accommodate an ambitious program of functional requirements, and he managed to fit seven stories behind a facade that reads as three.

At the entrance on 54th Street visitors are greeted by a lushly embellished mannerist portico flanked by a pair of carved, banded, and fluted marble columns. Beyond decorative keystones, the shields of the universities from which the club originally drew its membership (carved by Daniel Chester French and Keyon Cox), and artfully placed bronze balconies, the facade is enriched chiefly by crisp rustication and a stately cornice.

The arched windows facing Fifth Avenue offer passersby a glimpse into the red-and-gold members' lounge. Upstairs facing 54th Street is the club's vaulted library with elaborate murals by H. Siddons Mowbray. The top floor is occupied by the dining room. In between, on the mezzanine floors, are bedrooms, service spaces, and kitchens.

◈ 54th Street

While this stretch of Fifth Avenue was long dominated by the homes of the Vanderbilts, the Rockefellers laid claim to several blocks to the west. In 1884 John D. Rockefeller purchased the house at 4 West 54th Street from Arabella Worsham Huntington. While Rockefeller was as famous for his dislike of ostentation as the Vanderbilts were for indulging in it, his new house had, thanks to Mrs. Huntington, wonderful interiors. Several rooms survive, installed at the Metropolitan Museum of Art and at the Brooklyn Museum. Once settled on 54th Street, the Rockefellers took steps to protect their neighborhood from commercial encroachment by buying up adjacent land and encouraging their friends and associates to settle nearby.

❶ Philip Lehman House

7 West 54th Street
1900 · JOHN H. DUNCAN

Banker Philip Lehman's house is a classic Beaux-Arts dwelling with a central entry under a bowed balcony fronting two French windows, both with oversized cartouches. The attic stories and mansard are equally rich in their decoration. When Philip Lehman died in 1947, the house passed to his son, Robert, one of the great art collectors of the twentieth century. He filled the house with treasures and redid the interiors to provide an appropriate setting for his holdings. Today the collection has a special wing at the Metropolitan Museum of Art where some interiors have been recreated.

❶ James J. Goodwin House

9–11 West 54th Street
1896–98 · MCKIM, MEAD & WHITE

This house, a double residence built for Goodwin and his daughter, is an exact contemporary of the University Club. Here, instead of the Italian

Renaissance, the architects looked to eighteenth-century New England for their inspiration. The specific source is a Boston house by Charles Bullfinch. The result, happily intact, is a poised and pleasing composition in brick and limestone. Goodwin was an associate of J. P. Morgan. His son Philip was the architect of the Museum of Modern Art's first building on 53rd Street.

ⓚ William Murray Houses

13–15 West 54th Street
1896–97 · HENRY J. HARDENBERGH

This pair of houses was designed by the architect of the Plaza Hotel and the Dakota Apartments. The buildings share a substantial stoop and have nearly matching facades, including a mannerist-inspired fourth floor with elaborate keystones and strongly tapered pilasters. Number 15 has a deftly concealed extra story. In 1906 John D. Rockefeller bought number 13 for his son and his bride. The younger Rockefellers moved across the street in 1918 and John D. Jr.'s son Nelson moved in, using the house as an office for thirty years.

🄛 Rockefeller Apartments

17 West 54th Street

1936 · HARRISON & FOUILHOUX

The striking design of the building owes much to the friendship that developed between architect Wallace Harrison and Nelson Rockefeller during the construction of Rockefeller Center. Harrison was a devotee of contemporary European architecture, particularly the International Style. Rockefeller, also inspired by contemporary continental examples, was eager to build a new type of apartment house: open, airy, and light-filled. The target audience was executives seeking to live near their Midtown offices.

The result is an apartment building with no precedent in New York City: simple volumetric forms; smooth, unadorned wall surfaces; modern materials (painted steel casement windows and tawny brick); and above all, no applied decoration. The most distinctive features are the silo-like window bays rising nearly the full height of the building. 17 West 54th Street is one of a pair. A fraternal twin sits across an interior courtyard from it facing 55th Street.

It would be impossible to leave this Rockefeller-dominated neighborhood without mention of the Museum of Modern Art, which fills a substantial part of the south side of 54th Street between Fifth and Sixth Avenues. The museum dates to 1929 when Abby Aldrich Rockefeller and two friends established a small gallery devoted to contemporary art in rented space in what is now the Crown Building. In 1932 the Museum moved to a Rockefeller-owned brownstone on its present site. By 1939 additional lots along the block had been acquired and a new museum building by Phillip Goodwin and Edward Durrell Stone had opened. Over the years MOMA has been expanded repeatedly to designs by Philip Johnson, Cesar Pelli, Yoshio Taniguchi, Diller Scofidio + Renfro, and Jean Nouvel to become a complex that includes not just the museum and its sculpture garden but two apartment towers.

㉕ Gotham Hotel
(Peninsula Hotel)

696–700 Fifth Avenue
1902–5 · HISS & WEEKES

Facing each other across Fifth Avenue, the Gotham and St. Regis Hotels signaled the arrival of commerce in this once-exclusive residential neighborhood. They were among the first New York hotels conceived as "skyscrapers," and although they were designed for a wealthy clientele, their arrival was not welcomed by nearby residents.

Hobart Weekes ensured that his design harmonized with that of the University Club next door, on which he had worked as a draftsman at McKim, Mead & White. Cornices, balconies, and fenestration are closely aligned, and the scale of the rustication is carefully matched. The 20-story Gotham, however, is less restrained in its embellishment than the quietly dignified club next door. The exception is the entry portals, which are remarkably similar in style and detail.

㉖ St. Regis Hotel

699–703 Fifth Avenue
1901–4 · TROWBRIDGE & LIVINGSTON; 1927, SLOAN & ROBERTSON

By the turn of the twentieth century, John Jacob Astor IV's Waldorf-Astoria Hotel was showing its age and its location on 34th Street was no longer fashionable. Astor spared no expense on his new hotel, the St. Regis. It was planned to appeal to a wealthy clientele. Astor chose Trowbridge & Livingston, who were just beginning work on the B. Altman store, as his architects. In contrast to their sober Italian department store design, the architects here created a full-blown Beaux-Arts composition rising to an exuberant array of balconies, pediments, dormers, and a crested mansard. The brass and copper kiosk and the remarkable revolving doors under the entrance canopy on 55th Street are particularly glamorous touches.

Sloan & Robertson's addition to the east is tactful and subdued. This wing contains the King Cole Bar with its celebrated mural by Maxfield Parrish, moved here from its original location in Astor's Knickerbocker Hotel off Times Square.

㉗ Fifth Avenue Presbyterian Church

705 Fifth Avenue
1875 · CARL PFEIFFER; CHAPEL AND CHURCH HOUSE, 1925, JAMES GAMBLE ROGERS

Founded in 1808, this congregation moved north from its original home on Cedar Street in five stages. Carl Pfeiffer's building in New Jersey sandstone features a modest portal, some crisp and delicate Gothic details, and broad areas with little embellishment. There are, however, two dramatic towers. At nearly 300 feet, the southern one was the tallest in the city when it was completed.

The largely traditional Gothic exterior does little to prepare for the interior. A small vestibule opens not onto a nave and aisles, but into a broad, fan-shaped auditorium seating 1800 worshippers. The floor slopes downward to focus attention on the pulpit, and all sharp corners have been smoothed and curved to achieve unimpeded sight lines and good acoustics. Up above an enormous pipe organ is supported by an encircling gallery. The chapel behind the sanctuary, added in 1925, is a more traditionally ecclesiastical space. There is a vaulted apse with fine stained-glass windows, stone walls, and longitudinally arrayed pews.

㉘ 711 Fifth Avenue
(Coca Cola Building)

1927 · BETHLEHEM ENGINEERING CORPORATION

This dignified, sturdy office building was the original home of the NBC broadcasting empire and later housed Coca Cola's New York offices.

It was speculatively built by the Bethlehem Steel Corporation. There are fine bronze shop fronts and interesting pediments over the two entrance portals with their twin carved serpents.

㉙ Corning Glass Building

717 Fifth Avenue

1956–59 · HARRISON, ABRAMOVITZ & ABBE; UPDATED 1994, GWATHMEY SIEGEL & ASSOCIATES

The Corning Glass Building sits on an L-shaped lot that wraps around the back of 711 Fifth Avenue. The main entrance faces 56th Street and the building presents only a narrow facade to the Avenue. The designers have, however, elegantly orchestrated the massing and setbacks to dramatize the soaring 26-story slab tower. The suave use of green-tinted glass and aluminum for the curtain wall is a proud advertisement for Corning's products. The lower stories have been altered.

㉚ 712 Fifth Avenue

1907–8 · ADOLF S. GOTTLIEB

㉛ Coty Building

714 Fifth Avenue

1908 · WOODRUFF LEEMING; UPDATED 1991, BEYER BLINDER BELLE

712 Fifth Avenue was built as a commercial venture by the neighboring Fifth Avenue Presbyterian Church and does its best to look like an

eighteenth-century French townhouse. It is the first of a group of very handsome buildings that fill the remainder of the block moving north. For many years this was the home of the Italian publisher and bookseller Rizzoli.

Next door, the Coty Building long served as the American headquarters of the celebrated French perfume manufacturer. The architect, Woodruff Leeming, drew on contemporary Parisian prototypes for his elegant design. Virtually the entire facade is glass—a two-story shopfront below and three floors of small-paned windows above separated by steel mullions and spandrels. The upper windows incorporate decorative panels commissioned by Coty in 1912 from French glassmaker René Lalique. The clear, cast glass panels with their flowing art nouveau floral design are the only surviving example of Lalique's architectural work in the United States.

③② Trump Tower

725 Fifth Avenue
1979–83 · DER SCUTT

A shopping atrium, residences, and offices stacked within a dark and insistent 58-story tower. The building's most distinctive feature, the atrium with its acres of gilt and pink marble, sits beneath Scutt's "inverted pyramid of cubes" at the corner 56th Street.

⬦→ 56th Street

Ⓜ Frederick C. and Birdsall Otis Edey House

10 West 56th Street
1901 · WARREN & WETMORE

The key feature of this French-inflected design is the powerful and richly sculptural Palladian window with its oversized cartouche on the second level. The ground floor is modern. Financier Frederick Edey built this house as a gift for his wife, Birdsall Otis Edey, the suffragette and national president of the Girl Scouts.

Ⓝ Harry B. Hollins House

12–14 West 56th Street
1899–1901 · STANFORD WHITE OF MCKIM, MEAD & WHITE;
NEW ENTRANCE AND OTHER REVISIONS, J. E. R. CARPENTER

Stanford White produced a notably elegant and understated Federal home in brick and limestone for banker Harry Hollins. One originally entered the house through what is now the central window on the ground floor. The current entrance through a low wing to the east was created in 1924 when this was the home of the Calumet Club.

O Edith Andrews Logan House

17 West 56th Street

1870 · JOHN G. PRAGUE; REMODELED 1903–4, AUGUSTUS N. ALLEN

Another Federal-style house stands diagonally across the street. Architect Augustus Allen began with an existing brownstone residence. He removed the high stoop, relocated the entry to the center of the ground floor, added a Doric portico, and refaced the building in brick and limestone.

P E. Hayward and Amelia Parsons Ferry House

26 West 56th Street

1871 · D. & J. JARDINE; REMODELED 1907, HARRY ALLAN JACOBS

Little of the Jardines' original house remains visible. But the new facade added in 1907 is coolly impressive in the best neoclassical manner: crisp, flat unadorned planes, subtle proportions, and a carefully calculated interplay of solids and voids. When carved decoration is employed, as around the strongly rusticated entry on the frieze above, it is crisply and elegantly executed. A strong dark cornice closes the composition and masks the upper two stories of the original house.

Q Henry and Adelaide Seligman House

30 West 56th Street

1899–1901 · C. P. H. GILBERT

A grand French Renaissance mansion erected for the managing partner of the investment bank J. & W. Seligman & Company. Spanning two building lots and, thanks to the fifth-floor mansard, towering over its neighbors, the Seligman house is deliberately imposing. With the exception of the intricately carved balcony over the entrance and the detailing of the dormers, the design is comparatively restrained for a house that was clearly intended to make a statement.

33

33 Tiffany & Company

727 Fifth Avenue
1940 · CROSS & CROSS;
RENOVATION AND EXPANSION
2020–22, OMA

33

Tiffany's current home, its sixth building in Manhattan, is a solid and conservative late art deco cube. The restrained architecture foregrounds the famous display windows and their contents. The wonderful clock on the Fifth Avenue facade, supported by a nine-foot bronze figure of Atlas, is the visual highlight, moved here from the firm's previous stores downtown. A major renovation, currently underway, will include a new three-level penthouse with undulating glass walls. The 24-foot tall, column-free sales hall on the main floor with its coffered ceiling will remain.

Ten years earlier the same architects, Cross & Cross, replaced the Mary Mason Jones house across 57th Street from Tiffany's with a stripped down, modernized classical building for the New York Trust Company (737–741 Fifth Avenue). In recent years Louis Vuitton has taken over the lower floors and sheathed them in translucent glass.

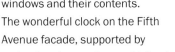

34 Hollander & Company Building

3 East 57th Street
1929–30 · SHREVE, LAMB & HARMON

Polished black granite frames a central screen of ribbon windows with embossed aluminum spandrels. Everything is sleek and elegant—exactly right for a store specializing in exclusive women's fashion. The parapet and crowning spandrels are particularly stylish, recalling details by the same architects at the Empire State Building and at 500 Fifth Avenue.

35 Heckscher Building
(Crown Building)

730 Fifth Avenue
1921 · WARREN & WETMORE

The architects described the style of this handsome set-back tower as "Francis I," and there is certainly an abundance of French Renaissance detailing here. In 1921 the building would have beautifully complemented the still-standing Vanderbilt chateau across the street.

Built of limestone, buff brick, and green-toned copper, the Heckscher Building featured rich stone and terra-cotta detailing on the lower floors and, notably, on the tower. Early critics rightly

compared it with that of the Woolworth Building. The original coloration, however, was understated. That changed in 1981 when former Philippine dictator Ferdinand Marcos secretly bought the building. He renamed it, added dramatic lighting, and proceeded to gild nearly every available surface. The upper floors are being converted into a hotel and residences.

㊱ Bergdorf Goodman

754 Fifth Avenue
1927–28 · BUCHMAN & KAHN;
ALTERATIONS 1984, ALLAN
GREENBERG

Tall pavilions facing 57th and 58th Streets flank a lower central section along Fifth Avenue. This facade, clad in white marble with contrasting bronze trim and a soft green slate mansard roof, is designed to resemble a row of townhouses. In 1984 the central section was redesigned by Allan Greenberg in heavily rusticated limestone to create a more prominent entrance for Bergdorf Goodman. In the process the original A-B-C-B-A rhythm of Ely Jacques Kahn's composition was lost at street level. Kahn's name is usually associated with art deco skyscrapers and lofts, but here to ensure that his building fit congenially with its neighbors, he chose a modernized French-inflected classicism.

㊲ Squibb Building

745 Fifth Avenue
1930–31 · ELY JACQUES KAHN; FACADE REPLACEMENT 1987, HAMMOND, BEEBY & BABKA

Here is Kahn in more typical form. The facade has been updated, but the original and very stylish entrance with its art deco screen and Arthur

Covey lobby mural remain intact. 745 Fifth Avenue was reputedly the architect's favorite design. He dressed up as the building for the 1931 Society of Beaux-Arts Architects Ball.

38

➌ Grand Army Plaza

1913–16 · THOMAS HASTINGS OF CARRÈRE & HASTINGS

In the original plans, Olmsted & Vaux indicated a plaza and carriage waiting area at the southeast corner of Central Park. Various designs for such a plaza were subsequently put forward, but the present scheme was adapted only in 1913 when Carrère & Hastings won a design competition prompted by a bequest from newspaper publisher Joseph Pulitzer. Pulitzer, who died in 1911, left $50,000 to erect a fountain "like those in the Place de la Concorde, Paris, France" on what was by then known as Grand Army Plaza.

This presented a design challenge since Augustus Saint-Gaudens's gilded equestrian statue of Union General William Tecumseh Sherman accompanied by a striding allegorical figure of Victory was already in place at the northern end of the plaza. The statue, on a base designed by Charles McKim of McKim, Mead & White, had been installed in 1903 under the auspices of the City's Chamber of Commerce.

Hastings' solution was simple and elegant. He placed his tiered Pulitzer Fountain with its crowning figure of Pomona by Karl Bitter to the south in front of the Plaza Hotel. Saint-Gaudens's monument was then moved slightly to the west so that the fountain and Sherman statue address each other across 59th Street.

39

🟣 Plaza Hotel

768 Fifth Avenue

1905–7 · HENRY J.
HARDENBERGH; 1921, ADDITION
ON 58TH STREET, WARREN &
WETMORE; MAJOR RENOVATION
AND PARTIAL CONVERSION TO
APARTMENTS 2005, COSTAS
KONDYLIS & PARTNERS

39

This is one of the great sites in New York—at the southeast corner of
Central Park, facing onto Grand Army Plaza and its fountain, and
overlooking Fifth Avenue. Probably inspired by Cornelius Vanderbilt's
chateau immediately to the south, Hardenbergh adopted a version of the
same style for the hotel. The central section of the two vast symmetrical
facades—one facing Fifth Avenue, the other Central Park—is executed
in white brick. At the 14th floor, however, the design breaks free into an
assortment of mansards, turrets, loggias, and dormers culminating in
a green tile roof. The building is a powerful and appealing anchor that
brings this key corner into focus, marking the transition from city to park
in an elegant and picturesque way.

In 2005 after several changes in ownership, a majority of the hotel rooms were merged and converted into condominium apartments and a food court was installed in the basement. At the same time, the original glass ceiling of the hotel's famous Palm Court was restored, and a number of other historic interiors were landmarked.

40 General Motors Building

767 Fifth Avenue

1964–68 · EDWARD DURRELL STONE WITH EMERY ROTH & SONS

The Plaza is one of New York's best-loved buildings, the General Motors Building less so. Set back from the street behind an open plaza, insistently vertical in its detailing, and incongruously stark in its material, the building remains aloof from its more traditional neighbors. As Ada Louise Huxtable pointed out at the time of the building's completion, it takes more than several tons of marble to make a Parthenon.

In contrast, Foster + Partners Apple Store (2018) is an elegant addition to the plaza in front. The store is entered through a coolly minimal, high-tech glass cube. Light penetrates to the stylish lower-level sales floor through 62 circular skylights punched thought the street level plaza.

Today Grand Army Plaza remains one of Manhattan's great public spaces—a gateway to Central Park and an elegant transition from New York's premiere retail neighborhood to its most glamourous residential quarter. At the same time, the buildings

surrounding the plaza present an appealing anthology of the work of great architects past and present, from Henry Hardenbergh and Charles McKim to Ely Jacques Kahn and Norman Foster.

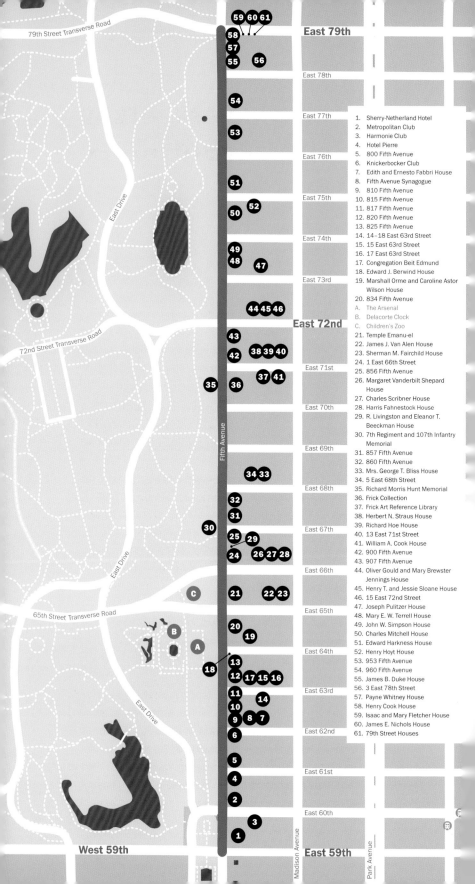

79th Street Transverse Road

East 79th

East 78th

East 77th

East 76th

East 75th

East 74th

East 73rd

East 72nd

East 71st

East 70th

East 69th

East 68th

East 67th

East 66th

East 65th

East 64th

East 63rd

East 62nd

East 61st

East 60th

East 59th

72nd Street Transverse Road

65th Street Transverse Road

West 59th

East Drive

Fifth Avenue

Madison Avenue

Park Avenue

1. Sherry-Netherland Hotel
2. Metropolitan Club
3. Harmonie Club
4. Hotel Pierre
5. 800 Fifth Avenue
6. Knickerbocker Club
7. Edith and Ernesto Fabbri House
8. Fifth Avenue Synagogue
9. 810 Fifth Avenue
10. 815 Fifth Avenue
11. 817 Fifth Avenue
12. 820 Fifth Avenue
13. 825 Fifth Avenue
14. 14–18 East 63rd Street
15. 15 East 63rd Street
16. 17 East 63rd Street
17. Congregation Beit Edmund
18. Edward J. Berwind House
19. Marshall Orme and Caroline Astor Wilson House
20. 834 Fifth Avenue
A. The Arsenal
B. Delacorte Clock
C. Children's Zoo
21. Temple Emanu-el
22. James J. Van Alen House
23. Sherman M. Fairchild House
24. 1 East 66th Street
25. 856 Fifth Avenue
26. Margaret Vanderbilt Shepard House
27. Charles Scribner House
28. Harris Fahnestock House
29. R. Livingston and Eleanor T. Beeckman House
30. 7th Regiment and 107th Infantry Memorial
31. 857 Fifth Avenue
32. 860 Fifth Avenue
33. Mrs. George T. Bliss House
34. 5 East 68th Street
35. Richard Morris Hunt Memorial
36. Frick Collection
37. Frick Art Reference Library
38. Herbert N. Straus House
39. Richard Hoe House
40. 13 East 71st Street
41. William A. Cook House
42. 900 Fifth Avenue
43. 907 Fifth Avenue
44. Oliver Gould and Mary Brewster Jennings House
45. Henry T. and Jessie Sloane House
46. 15 East 72nd Street
47. Joseph Pulitzer House
48. Mary E. W. Terrell House
49. John W. Simpson House
50. Charles Mitchell House
51. Edward Harkness House
52. Henry Hoyt House
53. 953 Fifth Avenue
54. 960 Fifth Avenue
55. James B. Duke House
56. 3 East 78th Street
57. Payne Whitney House
58. Henry Cook House
59. Isaac and Mary Fletcher House
60. James E. Nichols House
61. 79th Street Houses

CHAPTER 4

Along Central Park: Grand Army Plaza to 79th Street

The history of upper Fifth Avenue begins, not surprisingly, with the creation of Central Park. Olmsted and Vaux's Greensward Plan was adopted in 1857, and construction began two years later. By 1876 work was largely complete, including a broad, tree-lined walkway on the west side of Fifth Avenue. Even with these amenities, however, residential real estate development across from the park got off to a slow start.

In the 1880s Manhattan's social center of gravity was still firmly lodged in the 50s, centered on the Vanderbilts' Fifth Avenue mansions. Only a few bold pioneers built farther north. H. O. Armour erected a mansion at Fifth Avenue and 67th Street in 1880, and Ogden Mills followed with a house at 69th Street six years later. A crucial turning point came in 1893 when Caroline Schermerhorn Astor commissioned Richard Morris Hunt to design an impressive chateau on Fifth Avenue and 65th Street. Soon a flood of mansions appeared along the avenue itself and on the side streets to the east. Would-be residents had three choices: to commission a custom house designed from the ground up, to substantially renovate an existing brownstone, or to acquire one of the speculative houses being built by developers.

The houses along and adjacent to upper Fifth Avenue fall into three types reflecting the ambition and resources of their owners. At the top of the pyramid are freestanding mansions, set back from the street and occupying a full block. The Carnegie and Frick houses are the surviving examples. Next come corner houses, built with a narrow end on Fifth Avenue and the main front extending down a side street. Finally, there are the infill houses, built mid-block often as part of a row and presenting a narrow facade to the street.

A would-be resident could choose from a range of architectural styles. Their selection was influenced by favored historical associations, their choice of architect, and prevailing fashion. Many early patrons followed the example of the Vanderbilts and erected updated French chateaux, surely enjoying the implied association with French royalty. Richard Morris Hunt and C. P. H. Gilbert were recognized masters of the style. Those who followed the latest in Parisian architectural fashion might hire Carrère &

Hastings or Warren & Wetmore to build a house in a flamboyant version of the Beaux-Arts style, complete with a liberal application of cartouches and over-scaled ornament. Others might prefer an equally French house, but in a more restrained and historical mode. Ernest Flagg or Grosvenor Atterbury would be their architects of choice. A competing vogue for houses inspired by the palaces of Renaissance Italy was established in 1882 with the debut of the Villard Houses by McKim, Mead & White.

In the early twentieth century, fashion shifted to favor a cooler more classicizing taste inspired by eighteenth-century France. Horace Trumbauer and John Russell Pope excelled at such buildings. Finally, those who wished to celebrate their American heritage or who enjoyed the associations of eighteenth-century England could turn to Delano & Aldrich or McKim, Mead & White for a chaste red-brick and limestone home inspired by Federal or Georgian examples.

By the 1920s the economics of owning a Fifth Avenue mansion were becoming more and more challenging. Beginning with 998 Fifth Avenue and progressing with surprising speed, mansions along the avenue were demolished and replaced by large, handsome, and often very luxurious apartment houses. As was the case during the mansion boom, a comparatively small number of architectural firms designed the majority of the new apartment houses. Rosario Candela designed nineteen buildings along Fifth Avenue, and J. E. R. Carpenter designed sixteen, sometimes functioning as both architect and developer. Warren & Wetmore are similarly well represented. Between 1923 and 1929, fully one third of the avenue frontage facing Central Park was demolished and rebuilt as apartments. The Depression and World War II brought construction to a halt, but a new wave of apartment building began in the 1950s when most of the remaining mansions disappeared.

Many of the private houses on the side streets, along with a modest number on Fifth Avenue itself, have survived thanks to landmarking and zoning restrictions. Most have been converted for use as consulates, private foundation offices, galleries, or schools. Others have been subdivided into apartments, and a few continue as private residences.

❶ Sherry-Netherland Hotel

781 Fifth Avenue

1926–27 · SCHULTZE & WEAVER WITH BUCHMAN & KAHN

This 38-story apartment hotel was the world's tallest when completed. It is still one of the most appealing. Outside, the lower floors are clad in warm travertine and accented with ornate hanging lanterns. Step well back to take in the full drama of the tower with its loosely gothic pinnacle and crowning flèche. Inside, the groin-vaulted lobby simulates the hall of a Renaissance villa complete with frescoes and roundels salvaged from the Vanderbilt house that once stood diagonally opposite. Joseph Aruta's ceiling designs were inspired by Raphael's work at the Vatican loggia in Rome.

The Sherry-Netherland still falls just within Fifth Avenue's commercial district; hence the street-level shops. From this point, zoning prohibits commercial activity until 110th Street.

❷ Metropolitan Club

1 East 60th Street

1892–94 · STANFORD WHITE OF MCKIM, MEAD & WHITE; ADDITION 1912 BY OGDEN CODMAN

When a group of New York luminaries with names like Morgan, Vanderbilt, Whitney, Roosevelt, and Goelet found that some of their friends and associates had been excluded from membership in the Union Club, they started a new club of their own.

The architect described the style of this Italian palazzo as "severe and simple," and the building is indeed a considerable departure from White's contemporaneous home for the Century Association where every square inch of the exterior was adorned. Here the design relies on dignified proportions, crisp detailing, and impeccable craftsmanship to achieve its contained, imposing majesty. White did allow himself a flourish with the spectacular copper and marble cornice. It extends a full six feet from the building wall.

To ensure the visual integrity of the main block, White placed the entrance off a courtyard around the corner on 60th Street. It is guarded by a limestone screen with elaborate gates executed by the celebrated ironworker John Williams. The club interiors, including the double-height central hall sheathed in book-matched marble, are as lavish as the exterior is restrained.

❸ Harmonie Club

4 East 60th Street
1904–6 · STANFORD WHITE OF MCKIM, MEAD & WHITE

This is the second home of New York's second oldest club, founded by members of the city's German-Jewish community. Standing directly across 60th Street from the Metropolitan Club, the Harmonie is a careful, complex design, based like the Century Association on the Palazzo Canossa in Verona. Here, however, the composition is developed vertically rather than horizontally. The smooth, understated lower section of the facade is pierced by a classic Doric portico. The upper section is more richly detailed with a row of giant terra-cotta Corinthian pilasters supporting a fine cornice. A central recess with a shallow balcony is accented with a pair of Ionic columns.

❹ Hotel Pierre

795 Fifth Avenue
1929–30 · SCHULTZE & WEAVER

A few years after completing the understated, residential Sherry-Netherland, the same architects shifted gears. At the Pierre everything is grander, brighter, and showier. Designed to serve both residents and transients, the hotel quickly established itself as a center for social events and lavish entertaining. The lower floors are devoted to a carefully planned sequence of ballrooms and banquet halls. The tower was designed to recall the roof of Jules Mansart's chapel at the Palace of Versailles.

❺ 800 Fifth Avenue

1978 · ULRICH FRANZEN & ASSOCIATES

The bulk of 800 Fifth Avenue is a bland, mustardy-brick tower set back from the street. In front is a freestanding five-story limestone screen, a gesture to the historical structures nearby, holding the street and cornice lines as zoning required.

❻ Knickerbocker Club

2 East 62nd Street
1913–15 · DELANO & ALDRICH

Delano & Aldrich were pioneers in promoting the Federal style as an alternative for New York institutions, clubs, and mansions. The result here is restrained and patrician, very appropriate for one of the city's oldest and most exclusive clubs.

The building is a crisp red-brick box carefully outlined and delineated by limestone lintels, cornices, and a crowning balustrade. Simple, symmetrically arranged sash windows with six-over-six glazing add to the domestic aura and shallow balconies with elegant dark iron railings are tastefully deployed. Only at the entry with its broken segmental pediment and subsuming arch do the architects break loose a little.

🕖 Edith and Ernesto Fabbri House

11 East 62nd Street
1898–1900 · HAYDEL & SHEPARD; CONVERSION TO DIPLOMATIC USE BY PBDW ARCHITECTS

All the flourishes then popular in Paris are on display: exaggerated cartouches, sinuously curved balconies, giant pilasters, and sculptural panels. The double-width house was built for Commodore Vanderbilt's great granddaughter and was clearly designed to impress. The iron fence is particularly fine. Step back to enjoy the full baroque glamour of the facade and the lushly embellished dormers and tall chimney stacks piercing the mansard roof. Today this is the residence of the Japanese Ambassador to the United Nations. The architect was Augustus Shepard, Edith Fabbri's cousin. In 1916 the couple commissioned another house at 7 East 95th Street in a very different style.

🕗 Fifth Avenue Synagogue

5 East 62nd Street
1956 · PERCIVAL GOODMAN

The manner of worship here may be traditional, but the architecture is not. Through his careful choice of materials and attention to scale, the architect has demonstrated respect for the building's older neighbors on the block. For all of that, the 72 punched hexagonal openings on the facade, each containing a small stained-glass window, are indisputably of their era.

❾ 810 Fifth Avenue

1926 · J. E. R. CARPENTER

A classic 1920s building by the prolific Carpenter, 810 Fifth Avenue contains only twelve apartments. Here, as often the case with corner buildings, the entrance is on the side street, protected by a handsome metal canopy. The side-street entrance allowed ample park views from the principal rooms of the apartments. In 1968 when Richard Nixon and Nelson Rockefeller vied for the Republican Presidential nomination, both lived in this building.

❿ 815 Fifth Avenue

2020 · T. P. GREER ARCHITECTS WITH
THIERRY W. DESPONT

Tall, thin, cool, and aloof this private club/ condominium in white marble is an attractive infill building on the site of the former James Stewart Cushman house. Before its demolition, the house was the oldest remaining private building on this stretch of Fifth Avenue.

⑪ 817 Fifth Avenue

1925 · GEORGE B. POST & SONS

⑫ 820 Fifth Avenue

1916 · STARRETT & VAN VLECK

Two handsome and classic buildings from the great era of Fifth Avenue apartment building construction complement each other across 63rd Street. Both buildings begin with a rusticated base but at the fifth floor the masonry on 817 becomes smooth and flat. The original glazing has been replaced with flat, staring panes mounted close to the wall plane. Across the way, 820 Fifth is far more richly and sculpturally developed, retaining its rustication all the way to the cornice. Here the original six-over-six double-hung windows remain in place, adding to the building's warmth and plasticity. Both buildings feature large maisonettes facing Fifth Avenue. In many similar buildings, these have been converted to medical offices. Here they remain residences.

Just to the north J. E. R. Carpenter's handsomely massed **825 Fifth Avenue** ⑬, an apartment hotel from 1926, features an eye-catching wedge-shaped red tile roof and attractive set-back pattern.

East 63rd Street offers a neat illustration of the evolution of architectural taste in late nineteenth-century New York. The brownstone houses at **14–18 East 63rd** ⓮, two of which retain their original stoops, are typical of the buildings erected in the neighborhood in the 1870s. Across the street **Numbers 15** ⓯ (John H. Duncan) and **17 East 63rd** ⓰ (Welch, Smith & Provot), both built in 1901, signal the arrival of a new world, architecturally and socially. A major factor in this architectural and social evolution was the elimination of the tall stoop that was such a characteristic feature of the classic brownstone row house.

Brownstone visitors climbed the stoop to enter directly into a hallway on one side of the parlor floor. The remaining space on front of the house was occupied by a narrow parlor. At the rear there was a second parlor. The main family dining room was downstairs tucked beneath the stoop on the basement level. The kitchen was at the rear, opening onto a garden.

Around 1880, architects began to place the formal dining room at the rear of the parlor floor, linked to the kitchen below by a dumbwaiter. The high stoop vanished, and visitors now entered through a centrally placed door at street level leading to the main entry hall with a staircase leading up to the primary living floor, where the formal living spaces occu-

pied the full width of the building. This new planning strategy gave architects freedom to give each building an individual personality, to mix and match historical styles to suit evolving fashion and the tastes of their patrons. Without the stoop, facades could be moved forward to the building line, capturing valuable living space.

This block also features the elegant home of the Sephardic **Congregation Beit Edmund** ⓱, 11 East 63rd Street (1999–2003, Thierry Despont). The coolly classical building, built of limestone quarried in the Holy Land, is intriguingly asymmetrical. The facade is anchored by a pair of 18-foot bronze doors and is identifiable as a synagogue only by the single Star of David in the third-floor window.

⓲ Edward J. Berwind House

828 Fifth Avenue

1893–36 · NATHAN CLARK MELLEN

Berwind was a naval officer and capitalist, the largest individual owner of coal mines in the country. The Elms in Newport was his summer house. In the city he lived in this appealing red brick and limestone corner mansion, enriched with details borrowed from the palazzi of Renaissance Venice.

⓳ Marshall Orme and Caroline Astor Wilson House

3 East 64th Street

1900–3 · WARREN & WETMORE

Filling a double lot and designed in the latest French fashion, this house was built for the daughter of Caroline Schermerhorn Astor, who lived around the corner. The flat, unadorned wall surfaces are an effective foil to the ornate entrance portal, elaborate cartouches, and richly embellished mansard. Today the building houses New York's Indian Consulate.

❷⓿ 834 Fifth Avenue

1930–31 · ROSARIO CANDELA

During the 1920s and early 1930s, Candela was a highly sought-after designer of high-end luxury apartment houses. This 16-floor building offered a range of flats and duplexes from 3,500 to 10,000 square feet in size, plus several maisonettes with their own street-level entries. The apartments featured large rooms, tall ceilings, curving stairways, lavish entry foyers, and carefully considered plans.

Candela's exterior elevations are generally quite simple—here unadorned limestone with restrained art deco touches and a decorative

⬦ Central Park

Central Park is a constant presence along these blocks, providing residents not just with views from their windows, but with a place to experience the landscape. The perimeter walls of the park support a variety of monuments and memorials, and periodic gates offer access to the interior.

Vaux & Olmsted proposed unadorned openings in the low surrounding walls. Others, like architect Richard Morris Hunt, a champion of the City Beautiful movement, lobbied for large ceremonial gates on the European model. In 1862 Andrew Haswell Green, head of the Central Park Commission, stepped in with a compromise. Each of the entrances would be designated a "gate" named after a profession that contributed to the building of the park or after a segment of the population that used it. Originally there were eighteen gates, and Green chose the names and the openings to which they would be assigned with great deliberation. His choices are fascinating: Artists' Gate, Explorers' Gate, Hunters' Gate, Inventors' Gate, Warriors' Gate, Merchants' Gate, and even Strangers' Gate at 106th Street and Central Park West. Although the names were assigned in the 1862, signage identifying the gates was not installed until 1999.

Along Fifth Avenue are the Scholars' Gate at 60th Street, the Inventors' Gate at 72nd, the Childrens' Gate at 76th, the Miners' Gate at 79th, the Engineers' gate at 90th, the Woodsman's Gate at 96th, the Girls' Gate at 102nd, and the Pioneers' Gate at 110th Street. Additional entrances to the park were added in the twentieth century and are often unnamed, and some of the older gates were renamed or relocated by Robert Moses in the 1950s. At 65th Street, 79th Street, 85th Street, and 97th Street, sunken transverse roads allow traffic to move across town without disrupting the pedestrian paths and carriage drives within the park itself.

Ⓐ The Arsenal

830 Fifth Avenue, in Central Park at 64th Street
1847–51 · MARTIN E. THOMPSON

The Arsenal is one of two buildings in Central Park that predate the construction of the park itself. Resembling nothing so much as a fortified Tudor manor house (albeit with some eighteenth-century flourishes), the Arsenal is a solid and imposing structure with octagonal towers. It was originally built as a storehouse for arms and ammunition for the state militia. The city acquired the building in 1857 to house the 11th Police Precinct. The weather bureau arrived in 1869, and for eight years the building was the first home of the American Museum of Natural History. Today it houses the Parks Department. Inside the detailed historical murals depicting vignettes of New York during the Civil War in the main stair hall date to 1935–36 and are the work of Allen Saalburg.

Central Park Zoo

Olmsted and Vaux did not include a zoo in their plan for Central Park. Nevertheless, no sooner had the park opened than a menagerie spontaneously developed as members of the public began to donate exotic pets and other animals. A formal zoo was organized, and rudimentary buildings were constructed. Soon noise, odor, and crowding became an issue, leading to the establishment of a larger and better equipped facility in the Bronx. A large and popular selection of fauna, however, remained in the park. By the 1930s the facility was run-down. Parks Commissioner Robert Moses stepped in. With Federal support from the WPA the Zoo was beautifully rebuilt to designs of Aymar Embury. A much-needed update was undertaken in 1988 by Roche Dinkeloo.

Embury created and Roche retained a design featuring a series of pavilions arranged around a central pool. The grounds were richly embellished with specially commissioned works of art, including limestone friezes and bronze animals by Frederick Roth, Andrea Spadini and Edward C. Embury's **Delacorte Clock** Ⓑ and Paul Manship's handsome bronze gate to the **Children's Zoo** Ⓒ.

cornice above the rusticated base. At the setback level, the architect often created intricate terraces and exuberant penthouses. Water towers become small temples, buttresses and chimneys recall medieval castles. Here the upper sections are particularly quirky because the building was expanded to the south after construction was already underway.

㉑ Temple Emanu-el

840 Fifth Avenue
1927–29 · ROBERT D. KOHN,
CLARENCE STEIN, AND
CHARLES BUTLER

This is the home of the oldest Reform congregation in New York City (founded in 1845 on the Lower East Side), a building, particularly on the interior, of rare beauty and majesty. The exterior is an interesting blend of Romanesque and Moorish elements tempered by a good dose of art deco. The west facade is dominated by a tall, recessed arch with a rose window and a stepped arcade. Symbolic reliefs representing the twelve tribes of Israel decorate the arch and appear again on the fine gilt bronze entry doors. Down 65th

Street, attached to a community house, there is a handsome tower. It looks like a campanile, but houses water tanks and elevator machinery.

The interior is vast, seating 2,500 worshippers. The soaring column-free hall is flanked by narrow aisles with galleries. Marble is used lavishly as are Guastavino acoustic panels, set off with bands of shimmering glazed and gilded tile. Hildreth Meière created the mosaic arch framing the bimah. Other highlights include the twin Siena marble pulpits, the multicolored marble columns of the organ loft screen, and the vividly painted ceiling. The synagogue stands on the site of the chateau-style house of Caroline Schermerhorn Astor.

❷ James J. Van Alen House

15 East 65th Street
1916–17 · HARRY ALLAN JACOBS

This dignified Adam-style home with its bold, simple modeling and fine pedimented central Palladian window was built by Caroline Astor's son-in-law. Van Alen sold the house and moved to Europe in 1919 to protest Prohibition. Since 1945 this has been the home of the Kosciuszko Foundation.

❷ Sherman M. Fairchild House

17 East 65th Street
1941 · GEORGE NELSON AND WILLIAM HAMBY; NEW FACADE 1981, MILTON KLEIN

Aviation and photography pioneer Sherman Fairchild commissioned a house in an elegant and innovative version of the International Style with interior rooms grouped around a ramped three-story courtyard. The building was refaced in 1981 when it was converted into an art gallery.

㉔ 1 East 66th Street

1930–48 · ROSARIO CANDELA

㉕ 856 Fifth Avenue

1927–38 · ROSARIO CANDELA

Two Rosario Candela buildings—
one from early in his career,
the second from his final years.
One East 66th was designed in
1930, but due to the Depression
and World War II, was not
completed until 1948. The facade
is intricately sculptural and the
massing at the top is characteristically inventive. 855 Fifth Avenue is less
distinctive, but it does feature an attractive top-floor loggia.

One East 66th Street stands on the site of Charles Haight's imposing
house for sugar magnate H. O. Havemeyer and his wife, Louisine.
Demolished in 1930, the house contained not only the Havemeyers'
remarkable painting collection, much of which is now at the Metropolitan
Museum of Art, but also some of Louis Comfort Tiffany's most inventive
and sumptuously detailed interiors.

㉖ Margaret Vanderbilt Shepard House

5 East 66th Street
1898–1900 · RICHARD HOWLAND HUNT

Hunt's original inspiration may have been the
seventeenth-century Place des Vosges,
but he has fully embraced the lush taste of
fin-de-siècle Paris. The corbels supporting
the balcony, the iron work, and the parlor-
floor cartouches are wonderfully vigorous,
and the brick and stone color scheme is welcome in this neighborhood
where white limestone dominates. The building currently houses the
Lotos Club, a literary club founded in 1870 on Irving Place. Mark Twain
called it "The Ace of Clubs."

㉗ Charles Scribner House

9 East 66th Street
1909–12 · ERNEST FLAGG

Ernest Flagg built this house for his brother-in-law and patron, Charles Scribner. The building uses the same materials as Shepherd house next door, but here the detailing is far more delicate and classical. Note the fine carved rectangular panels beneath the third-floor windows and the elegant iron-fronted balcony above. Today the building houses the Polish Mission to the United Nations.

㉘ Harris Fahnestock House

13–15 East 66th Street
1918 · HOPPIN & KOEN

A rusticated ground floor with a symmetrical pair of entries is surmounted by two parlor floors tied together with colossal Corinthian pilasters and an attic above a fine cornice. The Fahnestocks moved out in 1941. In 1960 the building became the Consulate General of the Philippines. It was assigned to Imelda and Ferdinand Marcos "for their personal use."

㉙ R. Livingston and Eleanor T. Beeckman House

854 Fifth Avenue
1903–5 · WARREN & WETMORE

Despite being bookended by large apartment buildings, the Beeckman house still maintains its presence and poise. The house is only two windows wide, but those windows are grand with elaborate pediments on the parlor floor. At the third level, a cornice supports a double-height mansard flanked by two slab-like chimneys. The interiors are palatial. The building has long been the home of the Serbian Mission to the United Nations.

③⁰ 7th Regiment and 107th Infantry Memorial

Central Park at 67th Street

1927 · KARL MORNINGSTAR ILLAVA

Designed by a member of the 107th, the memorial honors the service of both regiments in France during World War I. The 107th Infantry was organized in 1917 as a spin-off of the well-known 7th (Silk Stocking) Regiment whose headquarters is the celebrated armory two blocks east on Park Avenue. The group of seven soldiers, depicted in action in France, is effectively dynamic in composition.

③¹ 857 Fifth Avenue

1963 · ROBERT L. BIEN

③² 860 Fifth Avenue

1950 · SYLVAN BIEN

After World War II, Fifth Avenue enjoyed a second apartment building boom. The new buildings were less lavish than those of the 1920s—fewer and smaller rooms, lower ceilings, and often no accommodation for live-in help. Many did, however, feature an innovation: private balconies. Most are bland compositions in white or beige brick, and many were designed by the father and son team of Sylvan and Robert Bien. 860 Fifth Avenue with its recessed central section is the work of Sylvan. Next door to the south Robert Bien spices things up with some Miami Beach/James Bond motifs: tall wavy piers facing 67th Street, deep insets on Fifth Avenue, and a projecting curved penthouse.

㉝ Mrs. George T. Bliss House

9 East 68th Street
1907 · HEINS & LA FARGE

This distinctive house is the work of the architects of the Bronx Zoo and the New York Subway system. The upper floors are a conventional Italianate essay in Roman brick. What sets the house apart is the monumental screen of Ionic columns on high bases that boldly tie together the ground and parlor floors. Inside on the main stair landing, La Farge included a magnificent stained-glass window designed by his father, John La Farge. The window is currently in the Metropolitan Museum of Art along with a room from the Hôtel de Crillon in Paris that was once incorporated in the mansion.

Next door, **5 East 68th Street** ㉞ was designed in 1894 by Boston architects Peabody & Stearns for real estate magnate John J. Emery. Sturdy and confident, the building is beautifully detailed. Note the porch, the second-floor window frames, and the fourth-floor rosettes and cornice. Today this is the home of the Indonesian Consulate.

㉟ Richard Morris Hunt Memorial

Central Park between 70th and 71st Streets

1898-1901 · BRUCE PRICE; SCULPTURE BY DANIEL CHESTER FRENCH

The Municipal Art Society erected this memorial to honor the first American architect trained at the École des Beaux-Arts in Paris. Hunt's portrait bust holds pride of place. To the sides are allegorical figures of Painting and Sculpture to the south and Architecture to the north. The latter figure holds a model of Hunt's Administration Building for the 1893 Chicago World's Columbian Exposition.

The site of the memorial was chosen because it was directly across Fifth Avenue from the Lenox Library, one of Hunt's most celebrated works. By 1912 the library collection had been transferred to the new New York Public Library and the Lenox building had been razed to make way for Henry Clay Frick's new home.

㊱ Frick Collection

1 East 70th Street

1913-14 · CARRÈRE & HASTINGS; 1935, JOHN RUSSELL POPE; 1977, JOHN BARRINGTON BAYLEY, GARDEN BY RUSSELL PAGE; RENOVATION AND EXPANSION 2021–23, SELLDORF ARCHITECTS

In 1911 industrialist Henry Clay Frick bought the entire block along Fifth Avenue between 70th and 71st Streets. He hired Carrère & Hastings, still at work on the New York Public Library, to create a very French mansion for his family and his growing art collection. Frick intended from the start that his house would eventually become a museum.

Occupying one of the highest sites along Fifth Avenue, Frick's house looks serenely at Central Park across a broad terrace. The original entry was through a carriage drive off 70th Street, the site of the current arched public entrance. When John Russell Pope was hired after Frick's death to convert the mansion into a museum, the drive was closed, and the former courtyard converted into a glass-roofed garden court. Additions to the north created a lecture room and expanded galleries. In 1977 the museum expanded to the east along 70th Street, adding a modest pavilion for visitor services and a viewing garden. The current

expansion by Selldorf Architects will include galleries for special exhibitions and make the second floor of the building publicly accessible for the first time.

At the request of Frick's daughter, Helen Clay Frick, Pope also created a separate but linked building on 71st Street to house the **Frick Art Reference Library** ❸. This imposing and severe structure with a monumental entry archway and careful Roman detailing was completed in 1935.

❸ Herbert N. Straus House
(Birch Wathen School)

9 East 71st Street
1930–32 · HORACE TRUMBAUER

Built for the son of Macy's owner Isidore Straus, this cool, formal building is among the last French neoclassical homes to rise on the Upper East Side. Straus, who died before he could move in, acquired several eighteenth-century French rooms for his interiors. Today two of these are in the Metropolitan Museum of Art.

39 **Richard Hoe House**

11 East 71st Street

1892 · CARRÈRE & HASTINGS

The Hoe house is fully as French as its neighbor, but far more spirited. Its early date also makes it something of an architectural pioneer. The detailing is wonderfully bold and crisp, and the overall composition of the facade open and well balanced. The treatment of the deeply set windows and the boldly figured marble columns flanking the entrance add drama and sculptural interest to the facade.

R. H. Robertson's Queen Anne residence for Eric Swenson at **13 East 71st Street** **40** dates from the same year as the Hoe house—two stylistic generations side by side.

41 **William A. Cook House**

14 East 71st Street

1912–13 · YORK & SAWYER

A Roman triumphal arch in white marble offers direct access at street level. The remainder of the three-story facade was inspired by Florentine palaces of the fifteenth century. The top floor loggia with its overhanging eaves is particularly evocative.

⓬ 900 Fifth Avenue

1958 · SYLVAN AND ROBERT BIEN

Another classic postwar building in light brick. Instead of their usual balconies, here the Biens feature two polygonal bays, trimmed in aluminum, that rise the full height of the building.

⓭ 907 Fifth Avenue

1915 · J. E. R. CARPENTER

907 Fifth anchors this prominent corner with dignity. This was the first apartment building to replace a standing mansion (the 1893 James A. Burden house) along Fifth Avenue. Carpenter was an investor in the building and owned an apartment here.

Across the way, the 72nd Street entrance to Central Park leads to the nearby Conservatory Water with its model boats and popular sculptures of *Alice in Wonderland* and *Hans Christian Anderson*. It's an easy walk to the Naumburg Band Shell and to the Bethesda Terrace overlooking the

Central Park Lake, a beautiful gathering place designed by Olmsted and Vaux.

㊹ Oliver Gould and Mary Brewster Jennings House

7 East 72nd Street

1898–99 · FLAGG & CHAMBERS

㊺ Henry T. and Jessie Sloane House

9 East 72nd Street

1894–96 · CARRÈRE & HASTINGS

Two remarkable survivors from the great era of mansion building, both beautifully restored. The Jennings house shows Flagg at his most opulent and Parisian. The composition is anchored by the solid rusticated ground floor and crowned by the exuberant curved mansard with its extraordinary copper cresting. Fine balconies with iron railings frame the calmer central section. The composition works beautifully and was clearly intended to blend well with its slightly earlier neighbor. From 1956 to 1959, while its Frank Lloyd Wright building was under construction, the Jennings House was the home of the Guggenheim Museum.

The Sloane House is even grander in conception. Above the rusticated ground floor with its dramatic cartouche-topped entry are two parlor floors with richly detailed windows linked by a stylish screen of Ionic columns. The composition is topped by a dormered mansard over a balustraded cornice. The Sloane House was built for the son of the founder of the W. & J. Sloane furniture firm. Over the years this was the home of James Stillman of the National City Bank, Joseph Pulitzer, and the Lycée Français de New York. Today both houses are owned by the Emir of Qatar.

Compared to this pair the next house, **15 East 72nd Street** ㊻, built in 1898 by John Duncan for Benjamin Guggenheim, seems quite modest.

⁴⁷ Joseph Pulitzer House

11 East 73rd Street

1900–3 · STANFORD WHITE OF MCKIM, MEAD & WHITE

Publisher Joseph Pulitzer's instructions to Stanford White were clear: "no ballroom, no music room, or picture gallery under any disguise ... no French rooms, designed or decorated to require French furniture ... I want an American home for comfort and use and not for show or entertainment." What he got was a Venetian palace, a characteristic White blend of the Palazzo Pesaro and Ca' Rezzonico. The house still seems to open onto the Grand Canal, but the beautifully detailed facade is less sculptural than the originals.

By 1900 Pulitzer was very nearly blind and extremely sensitive to sound. White made special models of the house for him to explore with his fingers, but he was unable to provide a sufficiently silent living space for his client. The publisher subsequently hired the firm of Foster, Gade & Graham to design a special double-walled soundproof annex. His staff dubbed it "the vault."

⁴⁸ Mary E. W. Terrell House

925 Fifth Avenue

⁴⁹ John W. Simpson House

926 Fifth Avenue

1898–99 · C. P. H. GILBERT

These two comparatively modest private homes for two separate clients were designed by the same architect. Although constructed from similar materials and using roughly the same design vocabulary, each house has its own distinct personality. Gilbert achieved a playful dynamic equilibrium across the two facades by varying the scale and placement of the two projecting bays and adjusting the fenestration. Both houses are still privately owned.

⑩ Charles Mitchell House

934 Fifth Avenue
1925–26 · WALKER & GILLETTE

By the mid-1920s the replacement of private mansions with apartment building was gathering steam, but the President of the National City Bank defied the trend. He built himself an impressive house, among the last to rise on Fifth Avenue. Walker & Gillette, who designed a series of branch banks for National City, were clearly channeling the Italian Renaissance at 934 Fifth Avenue. Compared with other nearby works of similar inspiration, however, the Mitchell House is a little dry.

The house served the Mitchells well as a setting for their elaborate social life and entertaining, at least until the stock market crash and some embarrassing financial investigations came along. Today the building houses the French Consulate, which has added an awning in the bright blue of the French flag with the address inscribed *en française*

⑪ Edward Harkness House

940 Fifth Avenue (1 East 75th Street)
1907 · JAMES GAMBLE ROGERS OF HALE & ROGERS

An elegant marble palace for one of the original partners in Standard Oil, the Harkness House breathes serene authority. The beautifully detailed building is set behind a particularly handsome iron fence protecting a light moat that admits sun to the two service floors. While the Italian palazzo exterior is luxuriously understated and stylistically consistent, the surviving interiors vary in inspiration, from Lorenzo di Medici to Louis XIV.

Some details to notice: the abstracted capitals that ring the rusticated ground floor (these top implied pilasters that are suggested by the breaks in the rustication); the finely corbelled window treatments on the parlor floor; and the meticulously carved cornice. Rogers went on to design residential colleges and academic buildings, including the Harkness Tower, at Yale University, as well as the Harkness mausoleum in Woodlawn Cemetery. Today the building is the home of the Commonwealth Fund.

❺❷ Henry Hoyt House

2 East 75th Street

1893 · RICHARD HOWLAND HUNT; EXPANDED 1910 AND 1919, HISS AND WEEKES

This red brick and limestone home presents an intriguing stylistic blend of the French and English. The basic inspiration is the French Renaissance, but some of the touches like the crest over the door are distinctly Tudor. The somewhat awkward stone-framed window at the third level once featured an oriel.

❺❸ 953 Fifth Avenue

1925 · ISAAC NEWTON PHELPS STOKES

Isaac Stokes was an author, public servant, and an architect. He co-authored the landmark 1901 *New York Tenement House Act* and later wrote the six-volume *Iconography of Manhattan Island,* an important compilation of documents relating to the early history of New York. A close ally of Fiorello LaGuardia, Stokes supervised the WPA mural

program in New York. He and his wife are the subject of a striking portrait by John Singer Sargent that is today at the Metropolitan Museum of Art.

At 953 Fifth Avenue Stokes's architectural solution to the challenge of a narrow lot was simple: take a standard mansion design and stretch it upward, inserting stories between the rusticated base and mansarded crown.

🞂 960 Fifth Avenue

1927 · WARREN & WETMORE WITH ROSARIO CANDELA

Built on the site of the infamously ostentatious William C. Clark mansion, 960 Fifth Avenue was one of the last super luxury apartment houses erected before the stock market crash. The building has two parts. The section facing the park contains a comparatively small number of apartments of unparalleled size and grandeur. Some had seventeen primary rooms and eight staff rooms. A second connected building, with its own entrance around the corner, has smaller units, but shared the in-house restaurant. The entrance off Fifth Avenue is sheltered by a particularly handsome glass and metal awning. The loggia on the tenth floor marks the location of Preston Pope Satterwhite's double-height, 58-foot-long living room.

The next block is a particularly distinguished one, the only one on Fifth Avenue that retains all its original turn-of-the-century buildings. This is due to the efforts of banker Henry Cook who in the 1870s purchased the entire block from 78th to 79th Streets between Fifth and Madison Avenues. Cook placed covenants on the building lots restricting construction to private homes.

⑤⑤ James B. Duke House

1 East 78th Street
1909–12 · HORACE TRUMBAUER; CONVERTED TO EDUCATIONAL USE 1959–60, VENTURI & RAUCH

Philadelphia architect Horace Trumbauer turned to the eighteenth-century Labottière mansion in Bordeaux for inspiration when commissioned by cigarette magnate James Duke to design his Fifth Avenue house. The results are impressive. The freestanding Duke house is poised and aloof, set back from the sidewalk behind a stone balustrade and basement well and separated from its neighbors to the rear by a garden. Visitors enter on 78th Street through an imposing rusticated two-story pedimented portico with flanking Tuscan columns. The whole composition is tied together with corner quoins. Duke's daughter presented the house to New York University in 1958 and Robert Venturi artfully converted the interiors for library and classroom use by NYU's Institute of Fine Arts. Inside, the central hallway and staircase are remarkable in their stately dignity.

Next door at **3 East 78th Street** ⑤⑥ the Edmund Converse Cogswell House (1897–99; C. P. H. Gilbert). It is a more modest version of the grand French Renaissance mansion that Gilbert was simultaneously building for Isaac Fletcher on 79th Street.

⑤ Payne Whitney House

972 Fifth Avenue

⑤ Henry Cook House

973 Fifth Avenue
1902–6 · STANFORD WHITE OF MCKIM,
MEAD & WHITE

These refined, architecturally linked
houses rise from a rusticated ground floor,
through a parlor floor detailed with engaged Iconic columns, to upper
floors of diminishing heights accented with Corinthian pilasters and a
final cornice. The forms are drawn from Italian Renaissance models but
scaled and adjusted to fit on Fifth Avenue. As always with White, the
detailing is assured and meticulous.

972 Fifth Avenue today houses the Cultural Services of the French
Embassy, including a fine French bookshop. The interiors are among
the architect's most sumptuous, particularly the so-called Venetian
Room, all gilt and mirrors—a space of wonderous spatial ambiguity. The
centerpiece of the circular marble entry hall is a fountain with a replica of
Michelangelo's *Young Archer,* acquired by the Whitneys for this spot. The
original is on loan to the Metropolitan Museum of Art. Outside, between
the Whitney house and the Duke mansion is the intimate Florence Gould
Garden, designed by Stan Allen and James Corner.

Although 972 and 973 Fifth Avenue appear to be a single building,
they have always been separate dwellings. 973 was built by the block's
developer, Henry Cook, after he sold his original house on the corner of
Fifth Avenue and 78th Street to James Duke. It is still a private residence.

⑤ Isaac and Mary Fletcher House

2 East 79th Street
1897–99 · C. P. H. GILBERT

Built for coal tar magnate Isaac
Fletcher and later occupied by
Harry Sinclair of tea-pot dome
scandal fame, this François I chateau is a real treasure. The composition
is romantically asymmetrical, but beautifully balanced. Large areas of

148

unadorned masonry set off the fine detailing surrounding the windows and particularly the sumptuously wide entrance portal. There are ogival arches, crockets, gargoyles, a full lexicon of late-Gothic features. The ensemble is topped off with a spectacular two-story slate roof pierced by dormers, chimneys, turrets, and pinnacles. A tiny conservatory is tucked off on the far left over the service entry. The Ukrainian Institute of America is the current owner.

60 James E. Nichols House

4 East 79th Street

1899–1900 · C. P. H GILBERT; REDESIGNED 1916, HERBERT LUCAS

Gilbert was a versatile designer. Just as he was completing the Fletcher house, wine merchant James Nichols commissioned him to create a lush Beaux-Arts house next door. Not much remains of the original design. It was updated by the next owner in a more severe taste. Just a trace of Gilbert's more richly ornamented style can be seen in the window treatments, cartouche, and cornice at the fourth floor.

The rest of the south side of 79th Street provides a handsome review of the architectural preferences of early twentieth-century mansion builders 61 . The Federal style of **Number 6** (1899–1900, Barney & Chapman) is followed by the imposing Beaux-Arts classicism of **Numbers 8** (1909–10; Henry C. Pelton) and **10** (1901, Grosvenor Atterbury) and the Roman brick Georgian style of **Number 12–14** (1901–3, Little & Brown). Henry Cook's covenant has ensured that none of these wonderful houses has been replaced by modern apartment houses.

East 110th

East 109th

East 108th

East 107th

East 106th

East 105th

East 104th

East 103rd

East 102nd

East 101st

East 100th

East 99th

East 98th

East 97th

East 96th

East 95th

East 94th

East 93rd

East 92nd

East 91st

East 90th

East 89th

East 88th

East 87th

East 86th

East 85th

East 84th

East 83rd

East 82nd

East 81st

East 80th

East 79th

Central Park North

West Drive

East Drive

97th Street Transverse Road

86th Street Transverse Road

79th Street Transverse Road

Fifth Avenue

Madison Avenue

Park Avenue

Lexington Avenue

3rd Avenue

1. 980 Fifth Avenue
2. 985 Fifth Avenue
3. Woolworth Houses
4. Mary Augusta King House
5. 993 Fifth Avenue
6. 995 Fifth Avenue
7. 998 Fifth Avenue
8. 1001 Fifth Avenue
9. Benjamin and Sarah Duke House
10. Metropolitan Museum of Art
11. 1014 Fifth Avenue
12. 1020 Fifth Avenue
13. 1025 Fifth Avenue
14. 1026 & 1027 Fifth Avenue
15. Jonathan and Harriet
    Thorne House
16. 3 East 84th Street
17. 1033 Fifth Avenue
18. 1045 Fifth Avenue
19. William Starr Miller House
    (Neue Galerie)
20. 1050 Fifth Avenue
21. 1056 Fifth Avenue
22. Henry Phipps House
23. 1067 Fifth Avenue
24. Solomon R. Guggenheim Museum
25. Archer M. Huntington House
26. Church of the Heavenly Rest
27. The Engineers' Gate/John Purroy
    Mitchel Memorial
28. Andrew and Louise Carnegie
    House/Cooper Hewitt,
    Smithsonian Design Museum
29. Otto and Addie Kahn House
30. James A. and Florence Vanderbilt
    Sloane Burden House
31. John Henry and Emily Vanderbilt
    Sloane Hammond House
32. William T. Stead Memorial
33. 1107 Fifth Avenue
34. Felix and Frieda Warburg House
    (Jewish Museum)
35. Willard and Dorothy Straight House
36. Mrs. Amory Carhart House
37. Ernesto and Edith Fabbri House
38. Ogden Codman Jr. House
39. Lucy Drexel Dahlgren House
40. Robert and Marie Livingston
    House
41. 1160 Fifth Avenue
42. St. Nicholas Russian Orthodox
    Cathedral
43. Mount Sinai Medical Center
44. Annenberg Building
45. Guggenheim Pavilion
46. Arthur Brisbane Monument
47. 1214 Fifth Avenue
48. New York Academy of Medicine
49. Site of former J. Marion Sims
    Monument
50. Museum of the City of New York
51. PS 171
52. Reece School
53. El Museo del Barrio
54. Conservatory Garden
55. Flower-Fifth Avenue Hospital
56. Lakeview Apartments
57. Church of St. Edward the Martyr
58. Charles A. Dana Discovery Center

CHAPTER 5

Museum Mile and Carnegie Hill: 79th Street to 110th Streets

At 79th Street, the mix of apartment buildings, mansions, and institutions along Fifth Avenue starts to change. This is the beginning of Museum Mile, one of the great concentrations of cultural institutions in the world. Beginning with the encyclopedic Metropolitan Museum of Art and continuing north to the Neue Galerie, Solomon R. Guggenheim Museum, Cooper Hewitt, Smithsonian Design Museum, Jewish Museum, Museum of the City of New York, El Museo del Barrio, and the Africa Center at 110th Street, the range of collections and exhibitions is remarkable. The buildings housing these institutions are just as impressive, ranging from classic Beaux-Arts temples to iconic modern masterpieces, from former mansions to purpose-built structures.

The blocks between 79th and 96th Streets also contain some of Manhattan's most prestigious apartment buildings. These tend to be more complex in design and layout than those to the south, with some buildings featuring intricate interlocking multi-floor plans. Similarly, private houses are more varied in style and personality.

North of 86th Street, the catalyst for private development was Andrew Carnegie's purchase in 1898 of a plot of land on Fifth Avenue between 90th and 91st Street, occupied at the time by squatters and a riding academy. Not only did Carnegie erect his own house at the top of what is now known as Carnegie Hill, he also purchased many of the nearby lots and then went on to determine what would be built and by whom.

Beyond 96th Street, the development of Fifth Avenue progressed more slowly. In 1911 when photographer Burton Welles issued his book *Fifth Avenue from Start to Finish,* he included images of every block from Washington Square north to 93rd Street. He stopped there because there was, in his view, little to show on the avenue farther north. In the years that followed, institutions such as Mount Sinai and Flower Fifth Avenue Hospitals, the Heckscher Foundation for Children, and the Museum of the City of New York moved in and came to dominate the northern blocks across from Central Park.

❶ 980 Fifth Avenue

1965–68 · PAUL RESNICK AND HARRY F. GREEN

❷ 985 Fifth Avenue

1969–70 · WECHSLER & SCHIMENTI

The demolition in 1965 of four nineteenth-century mansions built by the Brokaw family on the northeast corner of 79th Street and Fifth Avenue was a major catalyst for the creation of New York's Landmarks Preservation law. The two buildings that rose in their place are not the Avenue's finest: bland towers set back from the street line behind small plazas with curving automobile drop offs. They were built under recently changed zoning regulations that allowed developers to add extra stories to their buildings in return for the inclusion of the open plazas on their lots. In subsequent years, rules were adjusted to better protect the Fifth Avenue building line.

❸ Woolworth Houses

2–6 East 80th Street
1911–16 · C. P. H. GILBERT

Dime store magnate F. W. Woolworth commissioned C. P. H. Gilbert to build these houses, one for each of his three daughters. Woolworth's own mansion, across the street at 990 Fifth Avenue, was an imposing French Renaissance pile, strikingly similar to Gilbert's house for Isaac Fletcher one block to the south. Woolworth's house was replaced in 1927 by a handsome Rosario Candela-designed apartment house, but his daughters' houses survive in good condition.

❹ Mary Augusta King House

(American Irish Historical Society)

991 Fifth Avenue
1900–1901 · JAMES R.
TURNER & WILLIAM G. KILLIAN;
RENOVATIONS, 1911, OGDEN
CODMAN; 2006, JOSEPH PELL
LOMBARDI

Built on speculation by the developers John and James Farley, 991 Fifth was purchased upon completion by Mary Augusta King, widow of real estate tycoon Edward King. The American Irish Historical Society took over the much-deteriorated house in 1939 and returned the building to fine condition. In 2006 the interiors were restored based on Ogden Codman's original drawings from 1911. The building's three initial floors are handsomely bowed with strongly detailed arched French windows to illuminate the parlor floor. A fine iron balustrade marks the third level, and bold pedimented copper dormers pierce the slate mansard.

❺ 993 Fifth Avenue

1929–30 · EMERY ROTH

The exuberant entry portal here is balanced by an equally spirited crown—a stacked wedding cake of setbacks, terraces, and towers topped by red roofs. You need to step back into the park to enjoy it.

Roth, who designed such landmark buildings as the Beresford and San Remo on Central Park West, was also an apartment-planning pioneer. In his layouts he was careful to separate family, service, and entertaining areas. The latter were placed to enjoy the best views and were frequently organized to open off an oval lobby.

❻ 995 Fifth Avenue

1926–27 · ROSARIO CANDELA

This was originally The Stanhope, the only apartment hotel on Fifth Avenue north of the Pierre. For many years its Saratoga Room was a popular jazz and cabaret venue that hosted the likes of flutist Herbie Mann. This ended in 2005 when the building was converted to cooperative apartments. Unlike most contemporary Fifth Avenue apartment houses, the upper floors here are economically faced in brick, rather than limestone.

❼ 998 Fifth Avenue

1910–12 · WILLIAM SYMMES RICHARDSON OF MCKIM, MEAD & WHITE

This was the building that made apartment living socially acceptable to New York's upper crust. 998 Fifth contains only 17 units, a mix of flats and duplexes.

154

The design is calm, dignified, and majestic. 998 Fifth is essentially a stack of three superimposed Italian palazzi, separated by balconies and band courses. The lower section is rusticated; up above, the limestone walls are smooth ashlar accented with quoins. Each new section is introduced by one row of differently embellished windows—pediments on the second level, flat cornices on the third. Terra-cotta shields and a fine projecting stone cornice at roof-level enrich and complete the composition. The main entrance on 81st Street with its beautifully carved Renaissance frame is protected by an equally refined iron and glass canopy.

In order to entice the wealthy to forsake their mansions for apartment living, the developer of 998 Fifth, Douglas Elliman, offered former Secretary of State Elihu Root a substantial discount on a large apartment. Root relocated and was soon followed by former Vice President Levi Morton, Murray Guggenheim, and Mrs. Elliott F. Shepard, Commodore Vanderbilt's granddaughter.

❽ 1001 Fifth Avenue

1979–80 · JOHNSON/BURGEE

1001 Fifth is an awkward attempt to fuse the traditional and the contemporary. With its unbroken stacks of dark-trimmed and slightly bowed windows, 1001 is insistently vertical in a neighborhood where most buildings work to achieve balanced facades. Johnson's attempts to link his elevation visually to that of 998 Fifth Avenue to the south with broken string courses seem mannered, as does the crowning touch— the prominent fake mansard with its rear supports fully visible. Johnson was able to increase the height of the building beyond what zoning permitted by agreeing to forego street-level plazas.

❾ Benjamin and Sarah Duke House

1009 Fifth Avenue
1899–1901 · WELCH, SMITH & PROVOST

This striking and boldly colored house was originally one of four on this block built speculatively by developers William and Thomas Hall. Almost immediately upon its completion the house was purchased by American Tobacco Company co-founder Benjamin Duke, brother of James Duke of 1 East 78th Street.

The Beaux-Arts mansion presents a narrow front to Fifth Avenue. The main block extends down 82nd Street where the entry is marked by a dramatic glass and iron canopy at the base of a projecting bay. A deep light moat separates the house from the sidewalk. Above the limestone basement the body of the house is brick with vigorous stone trim and over-scaled pediments, cartouches, and brackets. The building is crowned by a tall mansard with corner pavilions pierced by dormers and accented with copper trim. While the main block is rigidly symmetrical in design, there is a small wing to the east with a projecting metal oriel window opening into a conservatory.

10

⑩ Metropolitan Museum of Art

1000 Fifth Avenue

1874–80, CALVERT VAUX & JACOB WREY MOULD; 1888, THEODORE WESTON (SOUTH WING); 1894, WESTON WITH ARTHUR LYMAN TUCKERMAN (NORTH WING); 1894–1902, RICHARD MORRIS HUNT & RICHARD HOWLAND HUNT (CENTRAL FIFTH AVENUE FACADE); 1905–26, MCKIM, MEAD & WHITE (FIFTH AVENUE WINGS); 1967–C. 2015, ROCHE-DINKELOO (MASTER PLAN AND ADDITIONS) CONTEMPORARY WING IN DESIGN BY FRIDA ESCOBEDO

Like the New York Public Library, the Metropolitan is one of New York's great Beaux-Arts landmarks. Unlike the library, however, the Met was not built as a single, coherent unit. This is a vast and complex building with a long and complicated architectural history.

In May 1869 New York State authorized the publicly financed construction of an observatory, a natural history museum, and an art museum within the confines of Central Park. Public and political wrangling followed, but in 1872 what would become the Metropolitan

Museum of Art was granted a parcel of land on the east side of the park at 82nd Street, between what was then a receiving reservoir and Fifth Avenue. The park's architects, Calvert Vaux and Jacob Wrey Mould, were commissioned to create a master plan for the new museum. The first section of their scheme was completed in 1880, a solitary and somewhat forlorn Ruskinian Gothic pavilion. In 1888 Theodore Weston added a more imposing brick and granite extension facing south; second similar wing to the north was completed in 1894. Today these buildings have been completely encased by later additions, but sections of the 1880 and 1888 facades can be seen inside the Lehman Wing and in the Petrie Court respectively.

In 1894 museum trustee Richard Morris Hunt was engaged to create an ambitious new master plan. This signaled a major change in the museum's architectural direction. The Victorian polychrome of Vaux, Mould, and Weston was set aside. Hunt embraced classical grandeur and reoriented the museum, turning it to face onto Fifth Avenue. The scale of the architect's vision can be seen in the monumental entrance pavilion at 82nd Street. Behind the confident and richly articulated facade is an entry hall of true Roman grandeur leading to a majestic stair that connects the pavilion to the original buildings.

In 1905 the architectural reins were passed to McKim, Mead & White. The firm revised and simplified Hunt's plan, adding five additional gallery wings and extending the facade a full 1,000 feet along Fifth Avenue. Low wings flank Hunt's entry, providing a link to dignified pavilions that frame the composition to the north and south.

Smaller additions by other architects followed until 1967 when Kevin Roche, John Dinkeloo & Associates were engaged to create another master plan for the museum. In the years since they have updated visitor circulation, created multiple new gallery wings (Temple of Dendur, Lehman Wing, etc.) and encased the museum on three sides with slanted walls of steel and glass that bring visual unity to the disparate components. In 2014 the Fifth Avenue plaza and fountains were reimagined by OLIN.

⑪ 1014 Fifth Avenue

1906–7 · WELCH, SMITH & PROVOST

Like 1009 Fifth Avenue half a block south, 1014 Fifth was built on speculation—by the same developers and the same architects. The result here is very different: a restrained and classic Beaux-Arts composition in limestone, rising from a rusticated ground floor to a copper mansard. The most distinctive feature is the pair of dished round-arched French windows fronting iron balconies on the parlor floor.

The house was purchased in 1910 by stockbroker James Clark. For many years this was the home of the New York branch of the Goethe Institute, a German cultural association. Today the building houses *1014–Space for Ideas,* a German-sponsored non-profit that seeks to "create a space to explore global challenges and opportunities." A major renovation by architect David Chipperfield is in the planning stages.

⑫ 1020 Fifth Avenue

1924–25 · WARREN & WETMORE

The exterior decoration may be understated, but the accommodations inside are not. Notice the asymmetrical arrangement of the windows facing Fifth Avenue. They reveal apartment layouts that are cleverly stacked and staggered to permit some to have salons overlooking Central Park measuring 20 by 40 feet with 18-foot ceilings. The top-floor duplex was long owned by the family of dime-store magnate and collector Samuel H. Kress, who filled it with Italian Renaissance art. His treasures are now divided between the National Gallery of Art in Washington and a number of university art museums.

⑬ 1025 Fifth Avenue

1955 · RAYMOND LOEWY,
WILLIAM SMITH

The low contemporary entry leads to a travertine and terrazzo corridor stretching eastward 100 feet to a pair of matching apartment houses, one facing 83rd Street, the other 84th. The buildings may be half a block off away, but thanks to this entry pavilion, they secured a coveted Fifth Avenue address. Designer Raymond Loewy's gateway is crisp and elegant: white marble frames a cantilevered concrete portico flanked by flower beds. The site was long occupied by a 1906 mansion, and its replacement leaves a disturbing void in the building wall along Fifth Avenue.

⑭ 1026 & 1027 Fifth Avenue

1901–3 · JOSEPH VAN VLECK &
GOLDWIN GOLDSMITH

⑮ Jonathan and Harriet Thorne House

1028 Fifth Avenue
1901–3 · C. P. H. GILBERT

The architects of 1026 and 1027 Fifth gave each of these handsome, speculatively built dwellings its own personality. At the same time, the two houses form a harmonious group that blends seamlessly with the contemporaneous Thorne house on the corner to the north. The buildings share the same broad steps, rusticated ground floor, coordinated balconies and cornices, and nearly identical mansard roofs.

The Thorne house, built for a leather-goods manufacturer, is in plan and elevation almost a clone of the slightly earlier Benjamin Duke house at 1009 Fifth Avenue. While the layout of the two buildings is similar, their style is not. The Thorne house, although hardly retiring, is far less flamboyant. Since the 1920s all three buildings have been owned by the Marymount School.

⑯ 3 East 84th Street

1927–28 · HOWELLS & HOOD

An art deco gem by a distinguished architectural team. The building was commissioned by newspaperman James Patterson, founder of the New York *Daily News* and a member of the family which owned, among other papers, the *Chicago Tribune*. In 1922 John Howells and his partner Raymond Hood entered and won a celebrated architectural competition with their design for a new Chicago Tribune Tower. Patterson was impressed, and he proceeded to commission multiple buildings from Howells & Hood. These included the headquarters of the *Daily News*, Patterson's country house, and 3 East 84th Street.

Hood's work here is every bit as stylish as his other buildings. Smooth slabs of limestone ashlar rise without interruption, separated by dark stacks of windows marked at each floor by decorated metal spandrels embellished with vaguely Mayan zig-zag motifs. To the east, the main block is visually balanced by a single column of bay windows.

⑰ 1033 Fifth Avenue

1870 · STEPHEN D. HATCH; REDESIGNED 1912, HOPPIN & KOEN

1033 Fifth Avenue is a survivor. Today the small private mansion, once the home of Iran's mission to the UN, is squeezed between large apartment houses. The house began life as one of a group of four brownstones designed by Stephen Hatch. In 1912 the house was acquired by publisher George Smith, who hired Hoppin & Koen to redesign the building in a more fashionable style.

⑱ 1045 Fifth Avenue

1967 · HORACE GRINSBERN

Masonry, either brick or stone, is the usual material of choice along Fifth Avenue. Here the designer tried something very different. Virtually the entire facade of 1045 Fifth is glass. The setback at the tenth floor smooths the transition to the Rosario Candela building at 1040 Fifth Avenue and the Miller house to the north. The penthouse here was once owned by Beatle Paul McCartney.

⑲ William Starr Miller House
(Neue Galerie)

1048 Fifth Avenue

1912–14 · CARRÈRE & HASTINGS; CONVERTED, 2001, SELLDORF ARCHITECTS

Even though architect Whitney Warren was his brother-in-law, William Starr Miller chose Carrère & Hastings to design his New York mansion. They did not disappoint, creating a striking and dignified building that would not be out of place on Paris's Place des Voges. The design achieves just the right balance of color and ornament, and its slightly attenuated proportions give the building a touch of extra energy.

After the deaths of Miller and his wife, the house was purchased in 1944 by Grace Wilson Vanderbilt, who lived and entertained there until 1953. Since 2001 the building has been the home of the Neue Galerie, a museum funded by Ronald S. Lauder and focused on German and Austrian art from 1890 to 1940. Annabelle Selldorf was responsible for the meticulous and sensitive renovation. Her treatment of the elegant central stair hall seamlessly incorporates Vienna Secession–inspired touches into the original design.

⑳ 1050 Fifth Avenue

1958 · WECHSLER & SCHIMENTI

㉑ 1056 Fifth Avenue

1951 · GEORGE F. PELHAM JR.

Two massive postwar buildings in beige brick. 1050 rises blandly for 14 floors before exploding into an elaborate composition of setback penthouses. The most interesting feature of 1056 Fifth Avenue is the stack

of cantilevered balconies that rise over main entrance. Like those at 860 Fifth Avenue, most of these have now been enclosed, compromising what was already a very busy facade composition.

㉒ Henry Phipps House

6 East 87th Street

1902–4 · GROSVENOR ATTERBURY

Built for Carnegie associate and philanthropist Henry Phipps, this has been since 1949 the home of the New York Liederkranz, a society dedicated to celebrating and performing German music. There is a statue of the muse Polyhymnia in the front garden. Atterbury's design draws heavily on the Venetian Renaissance. On the parlor floor round-arch casement windows open onto a finely detailed balcony. At the fifth floor, just under the crisp cornice, another row of arched windows with central oculi would be at home anywhere along the Grand Canal. Back at street level, there is beautiful original ironwork on the fence and front door.

㉓ 1067 Fifth Avenue

1917 · C. P. H. GILBERT

This was the second major apartment building (after 998 Fifth) to be built on upper Fifth Avenue. Gilbert here skillfully adapts his preferred French chateau mode to a tall building.

⓬ Solomon R. Guggenheim Museum

1071 Fifth Avenue

1956–59 · FRANK LLOYD WRIGHT; MAJOR ADDITION AND RENOVATION, 1988-92, GWATHMEY SIEGEL & ASSOCIATES

In the early 1930s, Solomon Guggenheim met the German painter Hilla Rebay. Under her insistent guidance, he shifted the focus of his art collecting to contemporary abstract art and began to consider the possibility of creating a museum to house his increasingly large holdings. The first Museum of Non-Objective Painting opened in temporary quarters at 24 East 54th Street in 1939, the same year in which the Museum of Modern Art opened its first permanent home nearby.

In 1943 Rebay convinced Guggenheim to hire Frank Lloyd Wright to design a permanent home for his museum. Due to the war and to subsequent material shortages, progress was slow, and Guggenheim died in 1949 before a design for the museum had been finalized. Several more years went by as his estate was being settled. Finally, in 1956 construction began under the auspices of the Solomon R. Guggenheim Foundation. In the end, the "temple" envisioned by Rebay and Wright— two visionary egomaniacs—took sixteen years to complete.

The design, which has its origins in Wright's early work, centers on a giant rotunda, an inverted ziggurat, containing a continuous ramp of skylit galleries. To the north, linked to the rotunda across a cantilevered slab, is a smaller "monitor" building that originally housed offices.

As dramatic, sculptural, and unexpected as the cast concrete exterior is, it is the interior that truly astonishes. After passing under the heavy low

portico, a soaring atrium explodes into view—rising 96 feet to the skylight. Around this airy core, the spiraling ramp provides constantly changing views. To one side are works from the museum's collection; to the other are vistas back across the atrium. Everywhere circles, cones, and triangles penetrate and interlock in a masterfully unified composition.

Over the years the Museum has faced pressing capacity issues and sought additional room both for both display and support activities. Given the unified and self-contained design of Wright's building, expansion was a challenge. Nonetheless, a number of alterations and additions were undertaken. The most dramatic of these is the tall vertical slab erected to the northeast by Gwathmey Siegel in 1992 as part of a comprehensive restoration of the Wright building. The exterior was restored again in 2008.

㉕ Archer M. Huntington House

1083 Fifth Avenue

1901–2 · TURNER & KILIAN; RENOVATION AND ADDITION, 1913–15, OGDEN CODMAN; RENOVATION 2021–22, ZIVKOVIC CONNOLLY ARCHITECTS

Railway heir Archer Huntington acquired this speculatively built house and immediately hired Ogden Codman to expand and renovate it. The result is a straightforward bow-fronted

French classical design. Inside Codman created a circular marble stair hall at the rear to link the Fifth Avenue house to a second mansion at 3 East 89th Street. In 1940 Huntington donated both houses to the National Academy of Design, which occupied the property until 2018. Today 1083 Fifth has been converted back into a single-family residence. The remaining Academy buildings around the corner have been taken over by an art gallery.

㉖ Church of the Heavenly Rest

1084–89 Fifth Avenue

1926–29 · HARDIE PHILIP OF MAYERS, MURRAY & PHILIP

This compact, powerful, elegantly stylized building was designed by the successors of Bertram Goodhue, who created so many notable New York churches (including St. Thomas's on Fifth Avenue). At first glance Heavenly Rest seems to have been carved from a single block of stone. Broad areas of unbroken limestone are pierced by large windows decorated with crisp delicate tracery that blend the Gothic and art deco styles.

Twin limestone towers facing Fifth Avenue flank a central portal with sculptural embellishment by Lee Lawrie. His figures seem to emerge organically from the fabric of the building itself. The church was originally intended to have a far more ambitious sculptural program (the tympanum of the main portal remains uncarved), but the stock market crash disrupted those plans.

Today the church's sculptural austerity is one of its most appealing features. Inside, the view down the broad unobstructed nave, flanked by

fine stained-glass windows, culminates in a stark, soaring stone reredos designed by Earl N. Thorp and a high rose window. Overhead is crisply executed vaulting in Guastavino tile.

On the 90th Street facade the architects have skillfully nestled the parish house into the tight space available to them, ensuring that light for the church's elevated eastern rose window is not blocked.

❷❼ The Engineers' Gate/John Purroy Mitchel Memorial

West side of Fifth Avenue at 90th Street

The Engineers' Gate is one of the major entry points into Central Park, providing cyclists with access to the looping park drive and runners with a ramp to the jogging path around the Jacqueline Kennedy Onassis Reservoir.

A memorial of John Mitchel is straight ahead. In 1914, at age 34, Mitchel was elected Mayor of the City of New York, the youngest person so honored. He served only four years, dying while training for service in World War I. This memorial, designed by Thomas Hastings and Donn Barber in 1928, features a bronze bust of the reforming politician by Adolph Alexander Weinman.

❷❽ Andrew and Louise Carnegie House
(Cooper Hewitt, Smithsonian Design Museum)

1090–99 Fifth Avenue (2 East 91st Street)
1899–1902 · BABB, COOK & WILLARD; CONVERTED FOR MUSEUM USE
1976, HARDY HOLZMAN PFEIFFER ASSOCIATES; INTERIOR RENOVATION
1995, POLSHEK PARTNERSHIP; MAJOR RENOVATION AND EXPANSION
2013–14, GLUCKMAN MAYNER ARCHITECTS, BEYER BLINDER
BELLE, AND DILLER SCOFIDIO & RENFRO; GARDEN REDESIGNED BY
WALTER HOOD

Andrew Carnegie's 1898 purchase of land on Fifth Avenue between 90th and 91st Streets was transformational. Suddenly what had been a remote and undeveloped neighborhood became fashionable. And because

Carnegie had bought up land to the north and south, he could be choosy about his neighbors.

In abandoning his house on 51st Street, the 70-year-old retired steel magnate moved north in search of air, light, space, and a garden. He envisioned a house that was "the most modest, plainest, and most roomy ... in New York." The result is not the most beautiful or elegant dwelling on Fifth Avenue, but it fulfills Carnegie's program. The building's aspect is rather dour and its detailing heavy handed, but it is spacious, with more than 64 rooms. The freestanding Georgian-style building resembles nothing so much as an English country house set in its own park.

The interior is rich and somber. A broad stair rises to the second level from an expansive wood paneled entry hall. Upstairs the highlight is the Teak Room, designed by American Aesthetic Movement pioneer Lockwood de Forest with carvings produced at his workshop in Ahmedabad, India.

In 1972 Carnegie's heirs gave the house to the Smithsonian Institution as a new home for the Copper Hewitt Museum and its remarkable collections of historic and contemporary design. Hardy Holzman Pfeiffer Associates converted the building for museum use. In 2013 the Museum embarked on a major renovation and expansion to add gallery, shop, café, and support spaces. The garden was renovated at that time and is now publicly accessible directly from 90th Street.

㉙ Otto and Addie Kahn House

1 East 91st Street
1913–18 · J. ARMSTRONG
STENHOUSE WITH C. P. H.
GILBERT

Only in New York could an English Georgian country house stand opposite a replica of the Palazzo della Cancelleria in Rome. Kahn was a hugely successful financier and one of New York's leading art patrons. His house is a building of dignity and simplicity, presenting an understated and symmetrical facade to the street. Behind that facade, the plan is more complex with a hidden courtyard and tower, a roof top terrace, and an enclosed porte cochère. The music room once played host to private concerts by, among others, Enrico Caruso and George Gershwin. Since 1934 the house has been the home of the Convent of the Sacred Heart School.

㉚ James A. and Florence Vanderbilt Sloane Burden House

7 East 91st Street
1902–5 · WARREN & WETMORE

The clear focus of the facade is the third level where three arched windows set in deep curved reveals behind elegant iron railings announce the location of the ballroom. Below are a dramatically rusticated ground floor and a small mezzanine, squashed under the weight of a balcony supported by oversized consoles. Up above at the fourth level, the attic windows are punched through the frieze below the cornice.

   The builder was a successful industrial iron founder, the world's leading producer of horseshoes. His wife, Florence, was the daughter of furniture magnate William D. Sloane and a Vanderbilt descendant. The house was a wedding gift from her parents. Today the Burden house has been joined to the Kahn mansion and is a part of the Convent of the Sacred Heart School.

㉛ John Henry and Emily Vanderbilt Sloane Hammond House

9 East 91st Street
1902–3 · CARRÈRE & HASTINGS

When Florence Burden's sister Emily was about to be married, their father bought this plot of land from Andrew Carnegie so that the sisters could remain neighbors. The architects of the two buildings coordinated carefully; both houses were originally entered from the side off a shared carriage drive. This is blocked today by a gate erected by the Hammond house's current tenant, the Russian Consulate. Like the Kahn house, the Hammond house is based on Italian Renaissance models and shares its fine proportions and beautiful detailing. The parlor floor windows overlooking 91st Street are particularly fine with their curved pediments and flanking Ionic pilasters.

㉜ William T. Stead Memorial

West side of Fifth Avenue at 91st Street
1920 · SCULPTURE BY GEORGE JAMES FRAMPTON; SETTING BY CARRÈRE & HASTINGS.

William Stead (1849–1912) was an influential English journalist and editor who perished on the *Titanic* after helping others into lifeboats. This affecting memorial, erected in 1920, is a copy of the original on the Thames Embankment in London. The flanking figures represent Fortitude and Sympathy.

❸❸ 1107 Fifth Avenue

1924-25 · ROUSE & GOLDSTONE

In the early 1920s developer George Fuller was eager to build an apartment building on land then occupied by the mansion of heiress Marjorie Merriweather Post. At first Post was reluctant to sell, but she agreed to do so on the condition that the new building include a mansion-sized apartment for her use. The result was what may still be the most lavish penthouse ever built in New York: a 54-room apartment with 17 bathrooms, two kitchens, and a dining room seating 125 guests occupying the top three floors of the new building. Post had her own private drive and entrance hall facing 92nd Street. Other tenants entered via Fifth Avenue. Post's apartment was long ago subdivided, but the tall Palladian window on the 12th floor overlooking Central Park marks the location of what was the main entry hall.

❸❹ Felix and Frieda Warburg House

(Jewish Museum)

1109 Fifth Avenue
1906-8 · C. P. H. GILBERT;
EXPANSION, 1989-93,
KEVIN ROCHE

Like the Isaac Fletcher house at 79th Street and the Woolworth house on 80th Street, the Warburg house is a subtly asymmetrical composition with much of the historicist detail concentrated on the upper floors. Broad areas of unadorned limestone set off the lushness of the François I decoration. As was usual with corner houses on Fifth Avenue, the main entrance is on the side street to open the view of the park over Fifth Avenue. Warburg was a collector, philanthropist, and a partner in the banking firm Kuhn, Loeb & Company. His wife was the daughter of Jacob Schiff, the firm's senior partner. Schiff initially advised his son-in-law to build in a less ostentatious style, fearing that too much display would incite anti-Semitic feeling. Warburg paid no attention.

Since 1947 the Warburg house has been the home of the Jewish Museum, an institution "at the intersection of art and Jewish culture." In the 1990s, the original building was expanded seamlessly to the north along Fifth Avenue by Kevin Roche.

This neighborhood is dominated by the work of J.E.R. Carpenter. Although not as well known as his contemporary and competitor Rosario Candela, James Carpenter (1867–1932) was the designer and sometimes the developer of a significant number of luxury apartment houses along Fifth and Park Avenues during the 1920s. While the exteriors are seldom remarkable, the apartments are notable for their generous dimensions and thoughtful layouts. Between 93rd and 98th Streets, Carpenter designed seven major buildings: 1115, 1120, 1143, 1148, 1150, 1165, and 1170; he is also the architect of the modest but charming 4 East 95th Street.

35 Willard and Dorothy Straight House

1130 Fifth Avenue

1913–15 · DELANO & ALDRICH

Diplomat and financier Willard Straight chose an understated Georgian mode for his home with subtle and pleasing results. Delano & Aldrich, who became specialists in the style, designed a crisp, poised, and assured building of considerable elegance. The coloristic and textural balance between the stone, brick, and dark wooden shutters is perfectly calculated, and the bull's eye windows on the fourth floor (probably inspired by those at Hampton Court Palace) give the building just the right touch of stylistic individuality.

36 Mrs. Amory Carhart House

3 East 95th Street

1913–21 · HORACE TRUMBAUER; RENOVATED AND EXPANDED, 2005, JOHN SIMPSON ARCHITECTS IN ASSOCIATION WITH ZIVKOVIC CONNOLLY ARCHITECTS

The Carhart house is cool and self-contained. As was the case with Trumbauer's Duke mansion on 78th Street, the inspiration was the

Paris of Louis XVI. The result is an ordered and formal eighteenth-century classical building, impeccably detailed. The brackets supporting the balcony and the handsome carved stone panels are worth particular attention. Long and appropriately the home of the Lycée Français de New York, the Carhart House has been converted into condominiums and expanded to the east. The new building is rigorously classical and includes both a new facade facing the neighboring courtyard and an elaborate penthouse designed to resemble a Roman temple.

㊲ Ernesto and Edith Fabbri House

7 East 95th Street
1914–16 · GROSVENOR ATTERBURY

This Italian Renaissance palazzo in warm brick with contrasting limestone trim could not be more different from the cool and aloof Carhart house. The L-shaped plan allows for a welcoming entrance courtyard overlooked by an enclosed loggia. Each floor has its own architectural personality with traditional prominence given to the *piano nobile*. The interior decor is fully consistent with the exterior, evoking that of a fifteenth-century Italian palazzo. This perhaps reflects the involvement of Egisto Fabbri, the owner's brother, who arranged the acquisition of a paneled library from a palace outside Urbino.

It is interesting to compare the 7 East 95th Street with the Fabbris' earlier residence at 11 East 62 Street (1899), one of the most flamboyantly baroque Beaux-Arts dwellings in the city. Clearly the couple's taste had shifted during a period of residency abroad. Since 1949 this has been an Episcopal retreat center, the House of the Redeemer.

❸❽ Ogden Codman Jr. House

7 East 96th Street
1912–13

❸❾ Lucy Drexel Dahlgren House

15 East 96th Street
1915

❹⓿ Robert and Marie Livingston House

12 East 96th Street
1916 · OGDEN CODMAN JR.

Ogden Codman Jr., who grew up in France and is perhaps best known for his collaboration with Edith Wharton on *The Decoration of Houses* (1897) an interior design classic, designed 7 East 96th Street on a Parisian model for his own use. He hoped that his residence would form the nucleus of a small group of similar French townhouses along both sides of 96th Street between Fifth and Madison Avenues, but only two were constructed.

❹❶ 1160 Fifth Avenue

1922–23 · FRED F. FRENCH COMPANY

An attractive low-rise building in an understated Adam style. The rooftop urns, iron

balconies, and low-relief sculptural panels on the Fifth Avenue facade are appealing grace notes. The building's comparatively modest size reflects an anomaly in Fifth Avenue zoning. In January 1922, reacting to concern about 12-story apartment buildings replacing townhouses, the city revised its zoning to limit the height along Fifth Avenue to 75 feet. Architect/developer J. E. R. Carpenter sued, and the zoning change was quickly reversed. 1160 Fifth Avenue was built during the short period when the 75-foot limit was in place.

㊷ St. Nicholas Russian Orthodox Cathedral

15 East 97th Street
1901–2 · JOHN BERGESEN

Built with contributions from Czar Nicholas II and with funds from across the Russian empire, St. Nicholas still serves as the Russian Orthodox Cathedral for the United States. The Finnish-born architect created a richly sculptural confection that fully embraces orthodox tradition. Dark brick, limestone trim, terra-cotta, copper roofing, and glazed tile draw the eye upward to a complex roofscape organized around five exotic and evocative bronze onion domes. The rectory to the west is skillfully integrated into the overall composition.

After the Russian Revolution, the building became hotly contested real estate as the church wrangled with the communist regime for ownership. Today religious authorities are firmly in control and have carried out a handsome restoration of the building.

㊸ Mount Sinai Medical Center

Mount Sinai owns this section of Fifth Avenue. The long-established hospital moved to this site from Lexington Avenue and 66th Street in 1904 seeking, like so many other institutions, light, space, and room to grow. Today the complex stretches from 98th to 102nd Streets and

east to Madison Avenue. Most of the hospital buildings fronting on Fifth Avenue such as the Klingenstein Pavilion, 1176 Fifth Avenue (1952; Kahn & Jacobs) are of only moderate interest, but there are some major exceptions.

㊹ Annenberg Building

1974 · SKIDMORE, OWINGS & MERRILL

This dark, brooding behemoth dominates both the neighborhood and even the view from Central Park. The building, faced in reddish Corten steel has a somber dignity, but does not deign to pay even scant attention to its surroundings.

㊺ Guggenheim Pavilion

1190 Fifth Avenue

1983–92 · PEI COBB FRIED & PARTNERS

The flat buff and gray brick facade holds the Fifth Avenue street line and respects established cornice heights. The base building extends eastward the full length of the block to Madison Avenue along 101st Street. Above this platform, separated by deep V-shaped indentations, are three 11-story towers. These are linked on the south by a pair of light-filled atriums topped with I.M. Pei's signature glass pyramids. The building is huge, but it is carefully detailed. There are crisp geometries and intriguing brick patterns wherever one looks. Refined design and understated materials create a composition that although cool and institutional is also dynamic and balanced.

ⓐ Arthur Brisbane Monument

West side of Fifth Avenue at 101st Street
1939 · RELIEF BY RICHMOND BARTHE; SETTING BY SHREVE, LAMB & HARMON

Arthur Brisbane was an influential newspaper editor, writer, and executive in the early twentieth century who worked successfully for both Joseph Pulitzer and William Randolph Hearst. Brisbane also formed a lucrative real estate development partnership with Hearst and erected Brisbane House across the street at 1215 Fifth Avenue (1925–26; Schultze & Weaver). He long occupied a three-story penthouse apartment here. The roof-top water tower, masquerading as a tile-roofed Renaissance loggia is particularly appealing.

ⓐ 1214 Fifth Avenue

2010–12 · PELLI CLARKE PELLI ARCHITECTS

At 50 stories, 1214 Fifth is the tallest residential tower on the Upper East Side. It abuts and is linked to a lower building on Madison Avenue housing medical offices and research facilities for Mount Sinai Hospital. The carefully composed tower with its angled and interlocking setbacks is elegant and transparent. The levels are linked by carefully placed vertical concrete panels that interlock with the horizontal floor slabs to create a lively pattern across the facades.

ⓐ New York Academy of Medicine

1216 Fifth Avenue
1925–26 · YORK & SAWYER

The Academy of Medicine is a health policy and advocacy organization and the home of an important library that counts among its treasures a model of George Washington's dentures, Sigmund Freud manuscripts, and one of New York's largest collections of cookbooks. The building's architects, York & Sawyer, are well known for their many New York bank buildings; and the Academy, a fortress-like palazzo, would make a fine financial institution. The most arresting aspects of the design are the handsome Romanesque entry portal with its tympanum relief depicting the Greek gods Asclepius and Hygieia, and the architect's choice of building materials. The two facades are a riot of seemingly randomly placed blocks of light and dark stone.

🄰 Site of former J. Marion Sims Monument

West side of Fifth Avenue at 103rd Street

South Carolina physician James Marion Sims (1813–1883) was long hailed as "the father of modern gynecology" and recognized as the founder of New York's first women's hospital. A monument to Sims was erected in Bryant Park in 1892. In 1934 it was relocated to this site opposite the New York Academy of Medicine.

In recent years as Sims's repellant practice of performing experimental surgeries on enslaved black women became better known, the monument became a source of increasing embarrassment. In 2018 city relocated the statue to Green-Wood Cemetery where Sims in buried and covered over the plinth. Work on a replacement by sculptor Vinnie Bagwell entitled *Victory Over Sims* is underway.

🄴 Museum of the City of New York

1220 Fifth Avenue
1929–32 · JOSEPH H. FREEDLANDER; RENOVATION AND REAR ADDITION 2006–8, POLSHEK PARTNERSHIP

The Museum's porticoed central pavilion facing Fifth Avenue is reached by a short flight of steps. To either side flanking wings and loggias frame

an attractive welcoming plaza. The building, in red brick with white marble trim, is rigidly symmetrical, poised, formal, and a little aloof. This is a history museum, and the Federal style was chosen to evoke both the English aspects of New York's heritage and the time when the city was briefly our nation's capital. The Museum was founded by the Society of Patriotic New Yorkers in 1923. It moved here from its first home, Gracie Mansion.

The bronze statues in niches facing Fifth Avenue date to 1941. They are by Adolph Weinman and depict two of New York's most influential early leaders: Alexander Hamilton and DeWitt Clinton. The museum's permanent exhibition "New York at Its Core" is smart and dynamic, a great way to learn about the city's history from 1609 to the present day.

51 PS 171

19 East 103rd Street
1899 · C. B. J. SNYDER

It would be impossible to over-state Charles Snyder's impact on the quality and design of New York's public schools. Snyder was Superintendent of School Buildings for New York City from 1891 to 1923, a period of explosive population growth. During his tenure, he designed more than 400 school buildings that are as remarkable for their technical innovations as for their grace and architectural ambition.

Snyder dramatically improved school fire safety, ventilation, and lighting while creating visually beautiful and inspiring environments for learning. His major innovation was the H plan, of which PS 171 is a fine example. The school building occupies the full depth of the block from 103rd to 104th Streets with open courtyards facing both the north and south. These were designed both to provide light and air to classrooms and as sites for safe student recreation. Tall windows illuminate each classroom and give the building a welcoming domestic air. Snyder adopted a variety of historical architectural styles for his schools from Collegiate Gothic to Dutch Colonial. Here his choice is a stripped-down version of French Renaissance.

⑤② Reece School

25 East 104th Street
2006 · PBDW ARCHITECTS

Across the street, a four-story glass curtain wall enlivened by scattered
colored panels is the defining feature of this light, airy, and welcoming
design for a school serving children with special needs.

⑤③ El Museo del Barrio
(Heckscher Building)

1230 Fifth Avenue
1921 MAYNICKE & FRANKE; RENOVATION 2009, IBI GRUZEN SAMTON

1230 Fifth Avenue was originally built by philanthropist Charles August
Heckscher as a home for abused and neglected children. The building
has been gradually transformed over the years into a city-owned cultural
center for the East Harlem Community. Since 1977 this has been the
home of El Museo del Barrio, a museum dedicated to the art and culture
of Latin America. The museum wing of the building contains a fine 600-
seat theater that at one time was a venue for both the depression-era
Federal Theatre Project and the New York Shakespeare Festival. The
theater interior is notable for its large and vivid murals by illustrator Willy
Pogany of scenes from children's literature. Stained-glass panels with
circus figures shade the ceiling lighting fixtures.

The Fifth Avenue courtyard was handsomely renovated in 2009. The
result looks very much like an updated version of the entry courtyard
at the Museum of the City of New York next door. Around the corner on
104th Street, the lobby entrance to the Capital Preparatory School of
Harlem has charming tile murals by ceramicist William Grueby depicting
children at play.

54 Conservatory Garden

Central Park between 104th and 106th Streets

1937 · GILMORE D. CLARKE AND M. BETTY SPROUT

This formal garden is one of Central Park's great treasures. The six-acre garden opened in 1937 under the auspices of then Parks Commissioner Robert Moses.

The imposing wrought-iron entry gate was designed by George B. Post for Cornelius Vanderbilt's mansion on Fifth Avenue at 58th Street. Inside, the garden is laid out in three sections. Facing the entry off Fifth Avenue is a yew-edged Italianate lawn framing a view to a fountain and a wisteria covered pergola. To the south there is a more intimate English-style garden with annual and perennial beds. Here a fountain honors children's book author Frances Hodgson Burnett with figures by sculptor Bessie Potter Vonnoh inspired by characters in her books. To the north is a more formal French garden that offers spectacular seasonal displays of annuals arranged around a central fountain celebrating philanthropists Samuel and Minnie Untermyer. Its centerpiece is a bronze sculpture by Walter Schott. Two handsome allées of crabapple trees separate the three sections.

55 Flower-Fifth Avenue Hospital
(Terrence Cardinal Cook Health Care Center)

1249 Fifth Avenue

1921 · YORK & SAWYER

The Flower Free Surgical Hospital (a component of New York Medical College) opened in 1889 on East 63rd Street as America's first teaching hospital. In 1938 Flower merged with the Fifth Avenue Hospital and moved into their building. In 1978 Flower-Fifth Avenue was in turn taken over by the Catholic Archdiocese of New York, which currently operates the facility as a short-term residential and rehabilitation center in association with New York Medical College.

The Hospital's X-shape plan with prominent corner pavilions embodied what were in 1921 considered best practices in hospital design. The layout maximized light and air, permitted the isolation of contagious patients, and allowed each of the four wings on each floor to be centrally supervised from stations at the "crossing." Flower-Fifth Avenue broke new ground by replacing traditional wards with private rooms. Note the handsome polygonal cupola and loggia where patients could enjoy fresh air and views. Opera fans will be interested to know that Maria Callas was born here.

56 Lakeview Apartments

1250 Fifth Avenue
1974–76 · CASTRO-BLANCO,
PISCIONERI & FEDER

This block-filling complex with nearly 1,000 low to moderate income apartments presents a bleak concrete block facade to Fifth Avenue, but the overall complex is carefully composed and features a pleasant interior courtyard.

⑤⑦ Church of St. Edward the Martyr

14 East 109th Street
1887 · GEORGE BAGGE; EXPANDED
1909, J. B. SNOOK

Since its founding in 1883, this tiny red-brick gem of a church has been a bastion of high-church Anglo-Catholic worship. The stained glass, along with the elaborately carved oak reredos with its crowing mosaic depicting Christ in Benediction, are by the celebrated firm of J & R Lamb.

⑤⑧ Charles A. Dana Discovery Center

Northeast corner of Central Park at 110th Street
1987–93 · BUTTRICK, WHITE & BURTIS

The section of Central Park north of 106th Street was not a part of the original Olmsted & Vaux plan.

In 1868 sixty-five acres of what was largely marshland were added to the park and transformed into an attractive landscape featuring a large irregularly shaped lake known as the Harlem Meer. As was the case at the larger Central Park Lake to the south, a boathouse was constructed. By the 1980s, decades of neglect had reduced this building to a shell. Rather than undertake repairs, the city commissioned a replacement. The new Harlem Meer boathouse is a wonderfully sympathetic contemporary interpretation of the original design. Today the building houses an information and education center.

1. 1280 Fifth Avenue/The Africa Center
2. Duke Ellington Circle
3. Arthur A. Schomburg Plaza
4. The Fifth Avenue
5. Martin Luther King Towers
6. Senator Robert A. Taft Houses
7. Engine Company 58/Ladder Company 26
8. 1400 Fifth Avenue
9. 1405 Fifth Avenue
10. 3 East 115th Street
11. Institutional Synagogue
12. Kalahari Condominium
13. Mount Morris Theater
14. 143 Fifth Avenue/8 West 118th Street
15. Fifth Avenue Partnership Homes
16. Shaare Zedek Synagogue
17. 1465 and 1473 Fifth Avenue
18. Fifth on the Park
19. 2 West 120th Street
20. Mount Morris/Marcus Garvey Park
21. Fire Watch Tower
22. 1–5 Mount Morris Park West
23. 6–10 Mount Morris Park West
24. 11–14 Mount Morris Park West
25. Harlem Presbyterian Church
A. 4–16 West 122nd Street
B. Holy Trinity/St. Martin's Episcopal Church
C. 220–228 Lenox Avenue
D. 200–218 Lenox Avenue
E. Temple Israel
F. Congregation Ukadisha B'nai Israel
G. 240–248 Lenox Avenue
H. 241 Lenox Avenue
I. 243–259 Lenox Avenue
J. Reformed Low Dutch Church of Harlem
K. Harlem Club
L. Harlem Library
M. 28–30 West 123rd Street
N. 4–26 West 123rd Street
26. John and Nancy Dwight House
27. 26–30 Mount Morris Park West
28. 32–34 Mount Morris Park West
29. Harlem Branch of the New York Public Library
30. National Black Theater
31. 28 West 126th Street
32. Rondinone Studio
33. Columbia Club/Fifth Avenue Hall/ Rhapsody on Fifth
34. St. Andrews Episcopal Church
35. 20 East 127th Street
36. St. Andrews Parish Hall
37. 2069 Fifth Avenue
38. 2064 Fifth Avenue
39. 2068–2076 Fifth Avenue
40. 17 East 128th Street
41. 15 East 128th Street
42. 12 West 129th Street
43. 17–25 West 129th Street
44. All Saints' Roman Catholic Church and School
45. Astor Row
46. Presbyterian Church of the Puritans
47. Fred R. Moore School, PS 133
48. 2150 Fifth Avenue
49. Lenox Terrace
50. Abraham Lincoln Houses
51. Riverton Square
52. Central Harlem District Health Center
53. Riverbend
54. Delano Village
55. 369th Regiment Armory

CHAPTER 6

Harlem: 110th Street to the Harlem River

At 110th Street, Fifth Avenue moves into Harlem, a radical change of character from its position as the setting for cultural landmarks and luxury residences downtown. Rather than defining the neighborhood, Fifth Avenue shifts to a contributing role as it travels north to Marcus Garvey Park, crosses 125th Street, and continues on to the Harlem River.

Until the 1870s this area was largely farmland, first settled by the Dutch and named for the small city near Amsterdam. Development, however, continued to press northward, and in 1873 the independent community became a part of New York City. Two years later, the completion of the first Grand Central Depot and track upgrades along what would become Park Avenue brought improved rail service on the New York and Harlem Railway. Soon El lines along Second, Third, and Ninth Avenues also linked Harlem to Midtown, making it possible for residents to commute to jobs downtown.

During the 1880s and early 1890s, speculative row houses sprang up all over West Harlem. The blocks along Fifth Avenue north of 120th Street, particularly those near Mount Morris (now Marcus Garvey) Park, were soon filled with substantial brownstones owned by political leaders, doctors, and other professionals. Churches, clubs, and civic buildings were erected nearby to serve the residents. The financial collapse of 1893 slowed construction, but by 1898 a second boom was underway, spurred by the anticipated arrival of the IRT subway. In 1904, just as the trains began to run under Lenox Avenue, the over-heated Harlem housing market collapsed, and landlords found themselves desperate for tenants. African American businessman Philip A. Payton Jr. saw an opportunity. He founded the Afro American Realty Company and assumed management of many struggling buildings in central Harlem. He guaranteed landlords above-market rents and recruited prosperous tenants from the Black community then being forced out of downtown districts by commercial development. Payton and other Black entrepreneurs soon purchased buildings themselves, just as the Great Migration was bringing thousands of African Americans north from the Jim Crow South. By the 1920s Harlem had become the vibrant cultural capital of Black America.

The development of southern Harlem followed a slightly different pattern. While the growth of a prosperous middle-class neighborhood around Mount Morris Park was well underway by the 1880s, the blocks along Fifth Avenue between 110th and 120th Streets remained a transitional area. Just after the turn of the twentieth century, the announcement of the subway project and the simultaneous displacement of thousands of residents from the Lower East Side by bridge and park construction made the area suddenly desirable. Developers rushed in, eager to erect apartment buildings before the provisions of the new Tenement House Act of 1901 came into force. By 1900 the neighborhood was well on its way to becoming the third largest Jewish community in the world with much of Fifth Avenue and the adjacent streets built up with tenements and modest apartment buildings.

With the onset of the Great Depression, formerly grand Harlem buildings began to deteriorate in a downward economic and social spiral that reached its nadir in the 1980s. Rather than make repairs many landlords abandoned their buildings. At one point the city owned nearly 65 percent of the real estate in Central Harlem. Several decades of aggressive urban renewal followed, and much of Harlem's nearly uniform low-rise cityscape was replaced with tall, isolated residential towers. Today nearly all the historic buildings along Fifth Avenue between 110th and 120th Streets are gone. Their replacements are an anthology of the varying approaches to subsidized and public housing in the late twentieth and early twenty-first centuries. The area around Mount Morris Park, now designated as an historic district, has seen many surviving brownstones lovingly restored. Further north is a mix of public housing, churches, and historic houses, a few dating to the years before Harlem was a part of New York City.

❶ 1280 Fifth Avenue/ The Africa Center

2012 · ROBERT A. M. STERN
ARCHITECTS

Over the course of several decades, the Africa Center (formerly the Museum of African Art) worked with a variety of partners to erect a new home on this site at the top of Fifth Avenue's Museum Mile. This mixed-use building is the result: an apartment tower on Fifth Avenue and a wing for the museum to the north. Distinctive trapezoidal fenestration marks the museum space within the larger structure. Galleries, designed by Caples Jefferson, are not yet complete, but the Center has initiated a lively program of lectures and events.

❷ Duke Ellington Circle

Intersection of Fifth Avenue and 110th Street

1997 · MARK K. MORRISON ASSOCIATES

In 1926 the traffic circle at the northeast corner of Central Park was named in honor of James J. Frawley, a Tammany politician. When in 1997 the layout of the intersection was redesigned as a shallow amphi-theater bisected by Fifth Avenue, it was renamed for the great composer and jazz musician Duke Ellington. (Some of the old street signs with Frawley's name still remain.)

A bronze memorial to Ellington by Robert Graham, erected at the initiative of pianist Bobby Short, adorns the western half of the circle. A dignified figure of Ellington stands beside a grand piano on a pedestal supported by columns decorated with caryatid figures of the nine muses.

Four leaf-scroll "Covington" lampposts remain in in place around the Circle. These fixtures, which once lined Central Park West and Central Park North, are increasingly rare. There were multiple designs for the Covington posts, but the leaf scroll pattern is the most elegant.

❸ Arthur A. Schomburg Plaza

1295 Fifth Avenue, Duke Ellington Circle
1975 · GRUZEN & PARTNERS WITH CASTRO-BLANCO, PISCIONERI & FEDER

This mixed-income housing project, sponsored by the New York State Urban Development Corporation, includes not just apartments but also commercial space, a daycare center, and landscaped public plazas. The roughly textured Brutalist concrete towers may not be subtle, but they provide an effective visual anchor at this crucial intersection. The paired balconies on alternating faces of the octagonal towers add visual rhythm and sculptural interest.

❹ The Fifth Avenue

1325 & 1330 Fifth Avenue
1989 · MOJO STUMER

These twin condominium buildings facing each other across the avenue carefully hold the street line and embrace the six-story height of classic New York tenements. The canopied main entrance is located mid-block, flanked by street level shops. Materials are modest and, aside from light brick quoins and string courses, embellishments are few, but the buildings have dignity and complement each other well. 1330 is also the home of the Harlem Academy, an independent day school.

❺ Martin Luther King Towers

1350–90 Fifth Avenue
1954 · WILLIAM I. HOHAUSER

❻ Senator Robert A. Taft Houses

1345–95 Fifth Avenue
1962–64 · DEYOUNG, MOSKOWITZ & ROSENBERG

These enormous public housing complexes are classic examples of early urban renewal efforts in New York. The key design influence was Le Corbusier's concept of "towers in a park" —tall apartment buildings set in superblocks surrounded by large areas of green space intended to provide ample light and air. In reality, such anonymous brick towers, built to accommodate the largest number of families at the lowest cost, became symbols of alienation and urban crime. By turning their back on the city's grid, the towers isolated residents from the life of the street and from the surrounding community.

The King Towers contain an impressive 1,872 apartments in the ten 13-story buildings. Improbably, the complex was originally named for song writer Stephen Foster. The name was changed in 1968. Across the way, the Taft Houses are designed as vertical slabs. The presence of yellow, blue, and green metal grills over the elevator cores separating the two wings of each tower provides visual relief to the unbroken walls of brick. Mature trees now provide a leafy canopy within the complexes and over the sidewalk.

❼ Engine Company 58/Ladder Company 26

1367 Fifth Avenue
1960 · ARCHITECT UNKNOWN

This crisp, spiffy firehouse set into the Taft project is a welcome surprise. Built of buff brick, with bright red doors, a hose drying tower, and a roof deck, the building is a tight abstract composition with a whiff of the nautical about it. New York City fire houses are typically set on side streets, but here Engine Company 58 is a welcome contributor to the Fifth Avenue streetscape.

❽ 1400 Fifth Avenue

2004 · ROBERTA WASHINGTON

This lively, if slightly top-heavy, composition in brick and cast stone combines street level retail with subsidized condominium apartments above. The L-shaped main block extends along Fifth Avenue and then turns the corner westward along 116th Street. There are additional larger units in lower buildings along 115th Street. This was one of New York's pioneering "green" buildings, made from largely recycled materials and incorporating geothermal heating.

Across the street at **1405 Fifth Avenue** ❾ and **3 East 115th Street** ❿ (2007), Washington has skillfully interwoven new construction with existing buildings to create a visually arresting composition that echoes the silhouette of 1400 Fifth. The

projecting elements on 1405 Fifth ease the visual transition from the enormous towers to the south back to the more domestic scale of the blocks ahead. Don't miss the copper cornice on 1413.

At the turn of the twentieth century, 116th Street was the center of Jewish life in Harlem. Most of the architectural reminders of this era have vanished, including the famous Congregation Ohad Zedek whose cantor Yossele Rosenblatt appeared (as himself) in the first talking motion picture, Al Jolson's *The Jazz Singer*. The sole survivor is the former **Institutional Synagogue** ⓫ (currently the Salvation and Deliverance Church) at 37 West 116th. The synagogue was long celebrated for its community and youth programs and included an indoor swimming pool.

Across the way the lively facade of the **Kalahari Condominium** 🄬 at 40 West 116th Street (2008; Frederic Schwartz) is enriched by bold graphics inspired by the those on the homes of the Ndebele people of South Africa. The building includes, in addition to apartments, a cinema and performance art facility, retail space, a daycare center, public parking, and outdoor recreation areas on the roof terraces.

🄭 Mount Morris Theater

(Teatro Hispano/Church of the Lord Jesus Christ of the Apostolic Faith)

1421 Fifth Avenue

1911 · HOPPIN & KOEN

Early in its life, this Edwardian-style movie house hosted overflow events from the Institutional Synagogue down the block. Later, during the 1940s, this was one of the rare places in New York where Spanish language films were regularly screened. Today the building, one of the few historic structures on this stretch of Fifth Avenue, is preserved as a church.

🄮 143 Fifth Avenue/ 8 West 118th Street

Canaan House Residential Project

1976 · NATHANIEL D. BUSH

Another tower-in-a-park housing project, but here the park has largely been filled in for parking (along 117th Street). The tower is unfortunately cut off from Fifth Avenue by a dreary row of low shop fronts. The cantilevered corners, popular in the 1970s, echo the form of the more upscale residential towers at Waterside Plaza by Davis Brody Bond.

⓯ Fifth Avenue Partnership Homes

East side of Fifth Avenue from 117th to 118th Street

2001 · DANOIS ARCHITECTS

The Partnership Homes are a laudable attempt to recreate the high-stooped brownstone row houses that once lined so many Harlem blocks: forty three-family houses, in red brick with cast stone trim. Each unit contains a large owner's apartment and two smaller rental units. The overall design and detailing are formulaic, and the shared stoops are ungainly, but the Partnership Homes go a long way to restoring a sense of neighborhood and community to this stretch of Fifth Avenue.

The Partnership Homes project fills the entire block extending to Madison Avenue. The houses facing on 117th and 118th Streets include spacious backyards, while off-street parking is available along two lanes behind the Fifth Avenue buildings. The entire site is handsomely landscaped.

⓰ Shaare Zedek Synagogue
(New Bethel Way of the Cross Church)

25 West 118th Street

1900 · MICHAEL BERNSTEIN

This curiously eclectic building is a relic from Harlem's Jewish past. Despite its dilapidated condition, there is real personality here. The facade is centered on a triple portal linked to a rose window above by a distinctively shaped panel with Moorish carving. The flanking towers feature similar Islamic-inspired reliefs and are topped with squared Tudor domes.

🔵 1465 and 1473 Fifth Avenue

2010 · MELTZER/COSTA & ASSOCIATES

Another block where old and new are skillfully interwoven. The contemporary structures by Meltzer/Costa incorporate multicolored brickwork and irregularly placed window openings to create a lively abstract composition that blends with the turn-of-the-century buildings to either side.

🔵 Fifth on the Park

1485 Fifth Avenue
2007 · FXFOWLE ARCHITECTS

The ground floor of this upscale building is more than a little flashy, but things settle down as the building rises. The detailing and coloration of the tower is crisp and careful. On the east side of 120th Street the architects have cantilevered apartments out over the roof of the older Bethel Gospel Assembly building to ensure that residents have a view of the park. The bronze sculptural group of the three women friends at the corner of 120th Street is by the Nigerian-born artist Nnamdi Okonkwo.

🔵 2 West 120th Street

1900 · GEORGE PELHAM

This classic turn-of-the-century apartment house is by a prolific designer whose buildings are dotted all over the Upper West Side and Washington Heights. 2 West 120th is lushly decorated, with red-brick walls playing off against boldly carved stone balconies, cornices, pediments, and other decorative elements. The composition is capped by a full copper cornice. The light wells and fire escapes reflect the impact of the Tenement House Act of 1901, which mandated such improvements.

⑳ Mount Morris/ Marcus Garvey Park

Most of the land in central Harlem is a flat low-lying plain. Mount Morris is a notable exception, a large stone outcropping that defied easy development. Recognizing this, the city purchased the land in the 1830s and created a 20-acre park named in honor of statesman Gouverneur Morris. In 1973 the park was renamed in honor of the activist Marcus Garvey, who encouraged a sense of Black pride and championed the Back-to-Africa movement.

Today recreational facilities, including a swimming pool, playgrounds and ball fields, and an amphitheater hosting concerts and plays, support the park's role as a vital community resource. The most notable architectural feature is the cast and wrought-iron **Fire Watch Tower** ㉑ (1855; Julius B. Kroehl) based on designs of the celebrated ironmaster John Bogardus. It's well worth a climb up the hill to enjoy the view over Harlem and to see the beautifully restored tower, the only remaining example of the many such towers that once dotted the city.

From the start the streets around Mount Morris have attracted upscale development. This is particularly true along the west side of the park, a safe distance from the noise and dirt generated by the railroad along Park Avenue. Albert Best, founder of Best and Company, and New York City Mayor Thomas Gilroy both lived here.

㉒ 1–5 Mount Morris Park West

1893 · GILBERT A. SCHELLENGER

㉓ 6–10 Mount Morris Park West

1891 · EDWARD L. ANGELL

Schellenger's houses are classic brownstone designs, with their original stoops intact. Note the bay windows, handsome terra-cotta detailing, richly embellished door frames, and fine cornice. Next door Angell added arched parlor floor windows, Flemish strapwork, and angled stoops. He substituted a line of engaged finials for the usual cornice.

㉔ 11–14 Mount Morris Park West

1887–88 · JAMES E. WARE

Ware's picturesque and personality-filled houses reflect the taste of a slightly earlier era. Brick and stone are contrasted more dramatically, deeply set windows emphasize the solidity of the walls, and each house has been provided with its own spiky gable. Applied ornament is largely restricted to the door frames. The group has great energy and variety, and the corner oriel remains whimsically charming, even if it has lost its conical roof and cresting.

🄯 Harlem Presbyterian Church

Mount Morris Ascension Presbyterian Church

16–20 Mount Morris Park West

1905–6 · THOMAS H. POOLE

The work of Thomas Poole, a British designer who specialized in Roman Catholic churches, is nearly always surprising and idiosyncratic. Harlem Presbyterian is an eclectic blend of classical, Romanesque, and Moorish motifs enlivened by assertively contrasting materials: rough-faced granite, smooth-cut stone trim, and yellow Roman brick. The architect even added an under-scaled and stylistically incongruous dome. The interior is, thanks to that dome and to the broad arched windows, bright and open with tall, fluted columns supporting a groin-vaulted ceiling.

⬦ 122nd Street, 123rd Street, and Lenox Ave

Harlem has traditionally been a neighborhood of churches and brownstones. Some of the finest are located in the beautifully preserved blocks just to the west of Marcus Garvey Park.

Ⓐ 4–16 West 122nd Street

1888–89 · WILLIAM B. TUTHILL

This unusually appealing row of brownstones was designed by the architect of Carnegie Hall. Note the rhythm of the alternating polygonal and rounded window bays, the elaborate stoops, and the intricate patterning of the cornice. The nearly contemporaneous row across the street (1887–88; Cleverdon & Putzel) takes a more classical approach to decorative detailing. That said, the curved stoops on Numbers 13 and 15 are quite remarkable.

Ⓑ Holy Trinity/St. Martin's Episcopal Church

18 West 122nd Street
1887–89 · WILLIAM A. POTTER

This is one of Harlem's finest churches, designed by a distinguished architect who also executed numerous buildings for Princeton University. The solid and boldly conceived Romanesque structure in rough-faced granite with brownstone trim has real power and dignity. Viewed from nearly any angle, the towers and gables overlap and coalesce into a satisfying composition. The church nave is placed parallel to 122nd Street and is entered through a transept. This unusual arrangement left room for a large symmetrically composed parish hall along Lenox Avenue. Today the church is closed, but preliminary exterior repairs are underway.

Lenox Avenue, which Langston Hughes called "Harlem's heartbeat," was designed from the start as a 150-foot-wide grand boulevard with a central median. It was named in 1887 in honor of philanthropist James Lenox. One hundred years later in 1987 it was rechristened for civil rights leader Malcolm X. Lenox Avenue was the center of community life during the Harlem Renaissance, and the blocks between 120th and 125th Streets retain wonderful buildings.

Just to the south of St. Martin's Church is a particularly handsome row of Romanesque and Renaissance houses (**220–228 Lenox Avenue ❻**, 1888–89; F. Carles Merry). While each building has a distinct personality, the row forms an elegant and coherent group.

In the next block, **200–218 Lenox Avenue ❼** between 120th and 121st Street (1887–88; Demeuron & Smith) demonstrates an alternative approach to row house design with mansard roofs pierced by dormers, crisply executed terra-cotta detailing, rich coloration, and fine brickwork. The French Renaissance moldings over the entry portals and round-arched windows on the parlor floor are particularly handsome.

ⓔ Temple Israel
(Mount Olivet Baptist Church)

201 Lenox Avenue
1906–7 · ARNOLD W. BRUNNER

The former Temple Israel was built
for a prosperous reform congregation with roots in Harlem dating
back to 1870. After Temple Israel relocated to the Upper West Side in
1920, Mount Olivet acquired the property.

 The building exudes seriousness and solidity. Four tall Ionic columns
flank recessed entry portals surmounted by arched windows below an
imposing cornice. Inside, the sanctuary is a high open box with galleries
and rich marble classical detailing. Stars of David still look down from
the fanlights above the stained-glass windows and the pedimented
marble ark is in place. Today its golden doors protect not the Torah but a
baptismal pool.

ⓕ Congregation Ukadisha B'nai Israel
(Ebenezer Gospel Tabernacle)

225 Lenox Avenue
1889–91 · CHARLES ATWOOD

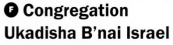

This building's complicated history
reflects the demographic evolution
of the neighborhood. The church
was erected by the Lenox Avenue Unitarian congregation, which occupied
it until 1919. At that point, it was sold to the Lithuanian Congregation
Chebra Ukadisha B'nai Israel. Finally, in 1942 it became the home
of the Ebenezer Gospel Tabernacle. The comparatively modest building
is thoughtfully designed, well-proportioned and built of well-laid brick
enriched with terra-cotta ornament. The south-facing gable with its twin
towers provides a solid visual anchor at the corner.

ⓖ 240–248 Lenox Avenue

1889 · JOHN E. TERHUNE

This handsome row of tall, stately houses features mansard roofs and

large windows simply framed in light-colored stone. Some have retained the checkerboard glazing in the upper section. The parlor floors are more richly embellished with bay windows, terra-cotta panels, and elaborate classically inspired entry porticos.

⊞ 241 Lenox Avenue

1883–85 · A. B. VAN DUSEN

⊙ 243–259 Lenox Avenue

1885–86 · CHARLES H. BEER

A beautifully intact row of stately brownstones. Van Dusen's house on the south corner is particularly grand in scale.

⊙ Reformed Low Dutch Church of Harlem
(Ephesus Seventh-Day Adventist Church)

267 Lenox Avenue
1885–87 · JOHN ROCHESTER THOMAS

The Gothic revival church's impressive size and soaring steeple make it a Harlem landmark. The proportions are a little awkward, and the yellow Ohio sandstone is an unusual choice for the neighborhood, but the building is a complex composition that repays attention. There are also some inventive capitals and corbels on the Lenox Avenue facade. A major fire in 1969 destroyed the interior, but the exterior was substantially rebuilt during the 1970s.

There is another fine row of smaller brownstones on the east side of Lenox Avenue north of 123rd Street (1885–87, Charles H. Beer). The great photographer James Van Der Zee, who chronicled Harlem life for half a century, had his studio at Number 272 from 1942 to 1969.

ⓚ Harlem Club
(ATLA World Missionary Church)

36 West 123rd Street
1888–89 · LAMB & RICH

Local bankers, brokers, lawyers, and merchants founded the Harlem Club in the mid 1880s "to cultivate friendly and social intercourse among its members, and to further and advance by means of concentrated action, matters of public welfare in the upper section of the City."

Lamb & Rich provided an imposing Queen Anne style clubhouse in brick and sandstone with terra-cotta ornament that features tall chimneys, prominent gables, whimsically detailed metal dormers, and a green tile roof. The composition remains imposing today, even in its somewhat neglected form. The Harlem Club survived only until 1907 when its finances collapsed. In subsequent years, the building housed a business school and a series of churches.

ⓛ Harlem Library
(Greater Bethel A.M.E. Church)

32 West 123rd Street
1891–92 · EDGAR K. BOURNE

The Harlem Library was founded in 1825 and occupied several buildings over the years. The style and elevation of its final home are carefully coordinated with that of the Harlem Club next door. Cornices and gables are matched and the library's arched entry portal echoes that of the club.

Competition from the New York Free Circulating Library (which did not charge for loans) brought about the merger of the two institutions and the eventual incorporation of both into the New York Public Library. In 1909 the Harlem Library collection moved into the new branch of the NYPL at 9 West 124th Street facing Mount Morris Park.

Ⓜ 28–30 West 123rd Street

1884–85 · JOHN E. TERHUNE

This matched pair of Queen Anne houses features beautifully blended brick and stonework embellished with delicate floral carving. The segmentally arched windows with their distinctive glazing are similarly elegant, and the entire composition is topped off with a dormer-pierced mansard. Each house is only 13 feet wide, but any lack of scale is made up in style.

Ⓝ 4–26 West 123rd Street

1880–82 · CHARLES BAXTER

Yet another dignified brownstone row, this time with incised neo-grec detailing. Number 4 stands out. A stylish oriel window was added around 1909.

26 John and Nancy Dwight House

31 Mount Morris Park West (1 West 123rd Street)
1889-90 · FRANK. H. SMITH

Built for the founder of the Arm and Hammer Baking Soda company, this was among the first Italian Renaissance inspired houses in Harlem. While not the most gracefully proportioned of compositions, the yellow Roman brick and deep copper cornice catch the eye. They pale, however, before the ornate Venetian entry portal.

For a number of years, the building housed the Harlem Arts Center and, subsequently, a branch of the Commandment Keepers, a congregation organized in 1930 by a Black rabbi, Wentworth Arthur Matthew. Since 2010 the house has been owned by writers James Fenton and Daryl Pinckney, who have restored much of the originally sumptuous interior.

26–30 Mount Morris Park West 27 (1880–81; A. B. Van Dusen) features interesting neo-grec detailing and unusually bold window lintels that cast dramatic shadows in the morning light. The handsome porticos are framed with appealingly simple Tuscan columns. In the next block **32–34 Mount Morris Park West 28** (1880–81; Charles Baxter) uses a similar architectural vocabulary but adds embellishments: fluted Ionic columns on the porticoes, more decorative window surrounds, and a strikingly vigorous cornice.

㉙ Harlem Branch of the New York Public Library

9 West 124th Street

1908–9 · MCKIM, MEAD & WHITE

This is one of a dozen Carnegie Libraries in New York designed by McKim, Mead & White. In 1899 the Carnegie Corporation provided a grant of $5,202,261 for the construction of 67 branch libraries in New York City. Nearly all the Manhattan libraries followed the same formula: arcaded ground floor with an off-center entry, main reading room on the parlor floor, and a third story for more specialized collections.

A block north of Marcus Garvey Park, Fifth Avenue crosses 125th Street, Harlem's main east/west thoroughfare. This has long been a major shopping street with important cultural institutions and good transportation. The Apollo Theater and Studio Museum are to the west, Metro North's Harlem railway station to the east. In recent years 125th Street has seen a significant revival with much new construction underway. A prime example is the **National Black Theater** ㉚ whose new home is currently under construction on the northeast corner of Fifth Avenue and 125th Street (2023–33 Fifth Avenue). Designed by Frida Escobedo and Handel Architects, the 21-story mixed-use building will house not just the theater, but also apartments and retail. David Adjaye's new building for the Studio Museum in Harlem is expected to open in 2024.

㉛ 28 West 126th Street

1871 · CALVERT VAUX AND FREDERICK CLARKE WITHERS; RESTORATION 1998, HAMLETT WALLACE

Built for Edward Gleason, Superintendent of the Union League Club, 28 West 126th is a rare surviving example of Vaux and Withers's domestic work. Vaux and Withers were key figures in the introduction of the English High Victorian Gothic style into America. While the house has lost its original mansard roof, the carefully laid deep red brick, contrasting white stone trim, and crisply incised carving of the door frame survive.

32 Rondinone Studio
(Mount Morris Baptist Church, Mount Moriah Baptist Church)

2050 Fifth Avenue

1887–88 · HENRY F. KILBURN; RENOVATION 2014, ALICIA BALOCCO

After serving as home to two Harlem congregations, this straightforward Romanesque church was sold in 2011 to Swiss artist Ugo Rondinone, who converted the building into a studio/home for himself. The building also includes two guest apartments and additional studio space for visiting artists.

33 Columbia Club/ Fifth Avenue Hall/ Rhapsody on Fifth

2056 Fifth Avenue

1902 · OSCAR LOWINSON; CONVERTED TO APARTMENTS 2008, BKSK ARCHITECTS

This unusual Beaux-Arts style building began life as a private club. In 1917 it became a community and political center for the large Finnish community that settled in the neighborhood following World War I. The Gospel Temple Church took over in 1955. Finally, in 2008 the building was converted to apartments and a distinctive diaper-patterned penthouse was added on the roof.

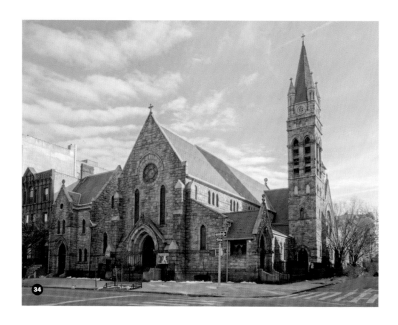

St. Andrews Episcopal Church

2067 Fifth Avenue

1872–73 · HENRY M. CONGDON
(ENLARGED 1889)

This is the distinguished and picturesque home of one of Harlem's oldest congregations, founded in 1829. The original church stood on East 127th Street between Park and Lexington Avenues, but in 1889 Congdon was hired to dismantle his building, enlarge it, and re-erect it on the present site.

The result is one of Harlem's handsomest churches: solid, rugged, and dignified. The slender and graceful tower with its open belfry and slate spire accented with corner turrets, is the design's most notable feature. Tucked into the angle of the transept along 127th Street, it provides a visual anchor to the long nave and leaves the Fifth Avenue frontage free for a single arched entry portal and bright red door. Note, as well, the smaller south-facing entry with its own vestibule, an inventive way to address the corner and balance the bulk of the tower. Walk down 127th Street to admire the building's bold and inventive detailing, especially the small, engaged tower with its peaked roof that smooths the transition from the buttressed main spire to the adjacent transept.

Across the street at **20 East 127th Street** ❸❺ (1869; Alexander Wilson) is a handsome early Harlem brownstone with its attractive Italianate details. From 1947 to 1967 this was the home of poet and activist Langston Hughes.

Back on Fifth Avenue, **St. Andrews Parish Hall** ❸❻ stands just north of church. Next door is the bright red brick facade and bold Queen Anne detailing on **2069 Fifth Avenue** ❸❼ (1909). It has a distinctive Flemish counterpart across the street at **2064 Fifth Avenue** ❸❽ complete with intricate terra-cotta embellishments. With the exception of the contemporary infill building next door, the rest of the block **(2068–2076**

Fifth Avenue) ❸❾ is occupied by an attractive row of townhouses. Even after some unsympathetic updating the group works as a unit, right up to the turret on the corner of 128th Street.

❹⓿ 17 East 128th Street

1864 · ARCHITECT UNKNOWN

This modest wood-frame building over a high brick basement is a picturesque survivor. Hundreds of such houses dotted Harlem before the building boom of the 1880s. Over the years 17 East 128th Street has been embellished with a fashionable Second Empire slate mansard roof pierced by dormers and some fine scrollwork under the eaves of the porch. **15 East 128th Street** ❹❶ next door displays some fine incised neo-grec detailing.

❹❷ 12 West 129th Street

1863 · ALTERATIONS BY EDWARD GUSTAVESON, 1883

Built when Harlem was still a suburban village, this was the home of two carpenters, William Paul and Thomas Wilson. The simple clapboard Italianate villa is freestanding, set well back from the street. The wonderful Moorish porch with its crisp scroll saw-cut trefoils and

quatrefoils was added by piano merchant John Bolton Simpson when he acquired the house in 1883. The original low attic was expanded to full height in 1896 when the building became a convent.

⑤ 17–25 West 129th Street

C. 1885 · ARCHITECT UNKNOWN

This lively group is a spirited demonstration of brick's possibilities as an alternative to brownstone. The English-inspired detailing is free and energetic, inventively blending brick, stone, and terra-cotta to dramatic effect.

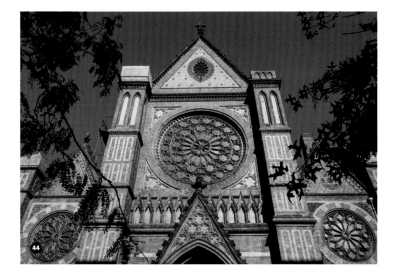

⑭ All Saints' Roman Catholic Church and School

Madison Avenue, 129th to 130th Street

1883–86 AND 1889–93 · RENWICK, ASPINWALL & RUSSELL; RECTORY/ PARISH HOUSE,1886–89; SCHOOL, 1902–4, WILLIAM RENWICK

This remarkably lively and energetic Italian/French Gothic design is the work of James Renwick, who also designed Trinity Church and St. Patrick's Cathedral. The overall plan and detailing of the church are first rate, and it would be hard to find a more impressive facade anywhere in New York City: a decorative and coloristic tour-de-force in brick, stone, and terra-cotta anchored by three large rose windows.

Around the corner facing Madison Avenue, Renwick's nephew designed the church's school building in his own variation on Venetian brick, stone, and terra-cotta. The main facade could not be more Italian with its careful balance of rich sculptural decoration and warm beige brickwork.

The parish was founded in 1879 specifically to serve an exploding, largely Irish immigrant population in the neighborhood. By the time of the building's completion, the congregation numbered over 5,000. Today the church has been deconsecrated and the complex has been acquired by a development group.

⑮ Astor Row

8–62 West 130th Street
1880–83 · CHARLES BUEK;
RESTORATION 1997, ROBERTA
WASHINGTON

This group of 28 matching houses was erected by William B. Astor Jr. on land that had been in the family since 1844. John Jacob Astor had acquired the plot as farmland and, as was family practice, the Astors held the property until the time was right for development.

Here the result is a modest and appealing row of simple, paired three-story brick houses, each set back from the street and graced by a welcoming wooden porch. Except for the porches, decorative detailing is almost completely suppressed, but courtyards between the buildings ensure that each has light and air.

⑯ Presbyterian Church of the Puritans

(St. Ambrose Episcopal Church)

15 West 130th Street
1873–78 · HUBERT, PIRSSON & CO.

In 1869 the Church of the Puritans sold its former home facing Union Square to Tiffany & Company, which demolished the building to erect a new store. The proceeds paid for this solid and impressive Gothic structure in rock-faced stone. There is a picturesque tower at the west, and a vestry nestled to the east of the nave with its own truncated tower. The Episcopalians moved in in 1936.

The **Fred R. Moore School, PS 133** 47 (1949) at 2121 Fifth Avenue is an attractive gently modern building named for the African American writer, newspaperman, and activist. Further along, note the exuberant baroque porch at **2153 Fifth Avenue** 48 complete with lion head brackets and a cherub.

Beginning immediately after World War II and continuing well into the late 1960s, the remaining blocks along Fifth Avenue were the focus of an intense program of urban renewal. Brownstones, tenements, businesses, and industrial properties were leveled and replaced with a sequence of apartment complexes arranged on superblocks. At first glance these tall tower-in-a-park brick boxes are almost indistinguishable from each other. Closer examination, however, reveals subtle variations. Each complex has a unique story and was designed to serve a specific clientele.

49 Lenox Terrace

West side of Fifth Avenue from 132nd to 135th Street
1957–60 · S. J. KESSLER & SONS

Six 17-story residential towers were built by a private developer with public financing. The buildings, although architecturally unremarkable, offer broad windows, individual balconies, landscaped grounds, welcoming lobbies, and uniformed doormen—all appropriate for the first upscale apartments to be built in Harlem in generations. Initial tenants included doctors, prominent politicians, and entertainers. To reinforce an aura of exclusivity, each building was given a suitably

upmarket name: The Buckingham, The Devonshire, The Americana, The Continental, and in a nod to the emerging popularity of Miami Beach, The Eden Roc and The Fontainebleau.

Across Fifth Avenue are the **Abraham Lincoln Houses 50**, a public housing project begun in 1948 and designed by Edwin Forbes, Vertner Tandy, and SOM as unmodulated brick towers were designed for lower-income families.

51 Riverton Square

East side of Fifth Avenue, 135th to 138th Street
1947 · IRWIN CLAVAN

Riverton Square was built by the Metropolitan Life Insurance Company in large measure as a response to criticism for its exclusion of Black tenants from Stuyvesant Town, its enormous middle-income development adjacent to the East River between 14th and 20th Streets. Described as a "separate but equal" development aimed at a middle-income Black clientele, Riverton Square encompasses seven 13-story brick buildings enhanced by gardens, playgrounds, and extensive plantings in the same vein as the complex downtown.

🟦 Central Harlem District Health Center

2238 Fifth Avenue

1936 · MCKIM, MEAD & WHITE

The Health Center is classic Depression-era public building: red brick, limestone trim, contained, unadventurous, loosely Federal in style.

At 138th Street Fifth Avenue is crossed by the traffic ramp leading off the Madison Avenue Bridge over the Harlem River.

🟦 Riverbend

East side of Fifth Avenue, 138th to 142nd Street

1967 · DAVIS, BRODY & ASSOCIATES

An alternative to the tower-in-a-park paradigm, Riverbend is a 624-unit middle-income complex composed of ten brick and concrete slab buildings of differing heights connected at the second level by open walkways and outdoor terraces. These create the sort of shared community spaces rarely found in public housing. Buildings are carefully placed to maximize light, air, and river views. Most units have private terraces and are inventively configured as duplexes.

   Aware of the cost of labor required to lay traditional bricks, the architects designed a larger brick to keep construction costs down. The shallow concrete balconies facing Fifth Avenue are an alternative to traditional fire escapes.

🟦 Delano Village
(now Savoy Park Apartments)

West side of Fifth Avenue, 139th to 142nd Street

1957 · MAXON, SELLS & FICKE

Another major housing project privately built but financed by the Federal Urban Renewal program. The seven brick towers set on a super block are architecturally unremarkable.

⑤⑤ 369th Regiment Armory

2366 Fifth Avenue

1921–24 · TACHAU & VOUGHT; ADMINISTRATION BUILDING, 1930-33,
VAN WART & WEIN

After the Civil War New York State mandated that each volunteer regiment have its own armory in which to gather, drill, and store equipment. In Manhattan today seven of these armory buildings survive in whole or in part. This is among the largest — the home of the celebrated "Harlem Hellfighters," founded in 1916 as the first African American unit of the New York State National Guard. The regiment gained fame for its valor in France during World War I and in the Pacific during World War II. Bill "Bojangles" Robinson was the unit's initial drum major and Vertner Tandy, New York's first registered Black architect, was at one time the regiment's commander.

The original drill hall on the west is of modest architectural interest, but the later administration building facing Fifth Avenue is an art deco

feast in red brick and terra-cotta with just the right echoes of a medieval fortress, the model for most earlier city armory buildings. In addition to its military role, the Armory has served as a homeless shelter and as the site for art exhibitions and athletic events. Today the Harlem Children's Zone operates programs there.

Just north of the stalwart armory Manhattan narrows, and Fifth Avenue, which began with such style at Washington Square, ends without ceremony, merging into the heavily trafficked Harlem River Drive.

To return downtown, the closest subway is the number 3 train, which stops at 145th Street and Lenox Avenue. The number 1 bus, stopping at Lenox Avenue and 142nd Street, will carry you all the way back down Fifth Avenue to Washington Square.

A Monograph of the Work of McKim, Mead & White. New York, 1915.

Adams, Michael Henry. *Harlem: Lost and Found.* New York, 2002.

Alpern, Andrew. *Apartments for the Affluent.* New York, 1975.

___. *The New York Apartment Houses of Rosario Candela and James Carpenter.* New York, 2001.

Bacon, Mardges. *Ernest Flagg: Beaux-Arts Architect and Urban Reformer.* Cambridge, 1986.

Bartless, Maurice Arthur. *Fifth Avenue.* New York, 1918.

Blake, Curtis Channing. *The Architecture of Carrere and Hastings.* New York, Columbia University (Ph.D. dissertation), 1976.

Bogart, Michele H. *Public Sculpture and the Civic Ideal in New York City, 1850–1990.* Chicago, 1989.

Boyer, M. Christine. *Manhattan Manners: Architecture and Style, 1850–1990.* New York, 1985.

Broderick, Mosette. "Fifth Avenue." In *The Grand American Avenue, 1850–1900,* ed. Jan Cigliano and Sarah Bradford Landau. San Francisco, 1994.

Brown, Henry Collins. *Fifth Avenue Old and New 1824–1924.* New York, Fifth Avenue Association, 1924.

Browne, Junius Henri. *The Great Metropolis, A Mirror of New York.* New York, 1869.

Burroughs, Edwin G., and Mike Wallace. *Gotham: A History of New York to 1898.* New York, 2000.

Chase, W. Parker. *New York, the Wonder City.* New York, 1932.

Devorkin, Joseph. *Great Merchants of Early New York: The Ladies Mile.* New York, 1878.

Dolkart, Andrew. *The Row House Reborn;*

Architecture and Neighborhood in New York, 1908–1929. New York, 2009.

___. *Touring Historic Harlem: Four Walks in Northern Manhattan.* New York, 1997.

___. *Touring the Upper East Side: Walks in Five Historic Districts.* New York, 1995.

Dunlap, David W. *From Abyssinian to Zion: A Guide to Manhattan's Houses of Worship.* New York, 2004.

Ellis, Edward Robb. *The Epic of New York City: A Narrative History.* New York, 2005.

Fifth Avenue Association. *Fifty Years on Fifth, 1907–1957.* New York, 1957.

Fifth Avenue Events: A Brief Account of Some of the Most Interesting Events Which Have Ocurred on the Avenue. New York, 1916.

Fifth Avenue Commission. *Preliminary Report of the Fifth Avenue Commission.* New York, 1912.

Goldberger, Paul. *The City Observed: New York, A Guide to the Architecture of Manhattan.* New York, 1979.

Granick, Harry. *Underneath New York.* New York, 1991.

Gray, Christopher. *Fifth Avenue 1911, From Start to Finish in Historic Block by Block Photographs.* New York, 1994.

Gura, Judith and Kate Wood. *Interior Landmarks: Treasures of New York.* New York, 2015.

Hammack, David. *Power and Society: Greater New York at the Turn of the Century.* New York, 1982.

Hawes, Elizabeth. *New York, New York: How the Apartment House Transformed Life in the City, 1869-1930.* New York, 1993.

Heckscher, Morrison. "Building the Empire City: Architects and Architecture." In *Art and the Empire City: New York 1825–1861,* ed. Catherine Hoover

Voorsanger and John K. Howat. New York, 2000.

Helmreich, William B. *The Manhattan Nobody Knows.* Princeton, 2018.

Henckels, Kirk and Anne Walker. *Life at the Top: New York's Most Exceptional Apartment Buildings.* New York, 2017.

Hendrickson, Robert. *The Grand Emporiums: The Illustrated History of the Great Department Stores.* New York, 1979.

Homberger, Eric. *The Historical Atlas of New York: A Visual Celebration of 400 Years of New York History.* New York, 2005.

Jackson, Kenneth T. (ed). *The Encyclopedia of New York City.* New York, 1995 .

Jackson, Kenneth T. and David S. Dunbar. *Empire City: New York through the Centuries.* New York, 2002.

James, Theodore. *Fifth Avenue.* New York, 1971.

Kathrens, Michael C. *Great Houses of New York, 1880–1930.* New York, 2005.

King, Moses. *King's Handbook of New York City.* Boston, 1893.

Koeppel, Gerard. *City of a Grid, How New York Became New York.* Boston, 2015.

Krinsky, Carol Herselle. *Rockefeller Center.* New York, 1978.

Landau, Sarah Bradford, and Carl Condit. *The Rise of the New York Skyscraper, 1865–1913.* New Haven, 1996.

Landau, Sarah Bradford. *Edward T. and William A. Potter: American Victorian Architects.* New York, Columbia University (Ph.D. dissertation), 1970.

Levin, Bernard. *A Walk Up Fifth Avenue.* London, 1989.

Lockwood, Charles, and Patrick W. Ciccone. *Bricks and Brownstone: The New York Row House.* New York, 2019.

Lockwood, Charles. *Manhattan Moves Uptown: An Illustrated History.* Boston, 1976.

Miller, Tom. *Seeking New York: The Stories Behind the Historic Architecture of Manhattan One Building at a Time.* New York, 2015.

Nash, Eric. *Manhattan Skyscrapers.* New York, 2005.

Ogden, Oliver J. *New York's Fifh Avenue Coach Company, 1885–1960.* Hudson, WI, 2009.

Ossman, Laurie and Heather Ewing. *Carrere and Hastings: The Masterworks.* New York, 2011.

Page, Max. *The Creative Destruction of Manhattan, 1900–1940.* New York, 1999.

Patterson, Jerry. *Fifth Avenue: The Best Address.* New York, 1998.

Pennoyer, Peter, and Anne Walker. *The Architecture of Delano and Aldrich.* New York, 1998.

___. *The Architecture of Warren and Wetmore.* New York, 2006.

Plunz, Richard. *A History of Housing in New York City.* New York, 2016.

Reed, Henry Hope. *The New York Public Library: Its Architecture and Decoration.* New York, 1986.

Robins, Anthony W. *New York Art Deco: A Guide to Gotham's Jazz Age Architecture.* New York, 2017.

Robinson, Cervin, and Rosemary Haag Bletter. *Skyscraper Style: Art Deco New York.* New York, 1975.

Rothermell, Fred. *Fifth Avenue: Twenty Eight X-Rays of a Street.* New York, 1930.

Ruttenberger, Steven. *Mansions in the Clouds: The Skyscraper Palazzi of Emery Roth.* New York, 1986.

Sharp, Lewis I. *New York Public Sculpture by 19th-Century American Artists.* New York, 1974.

Simon, Kate. *Fifth Avenue: A Very Social Story.* New York, 1978.

Stern, Robert A. M., David Fishman, and Jacob Tilove. *New York 2000: Architecture and Urbanism Between the Bicentennial and the Milennium.* New York, 2006.

Stern, Robert A. M., Gregory Gilmartin, and John Montague Massengale. *New York 1900, Metropolitan Architecture and Urbanism 1890–1915.* New York, 1983.

Stern, Robert A. M., Gregory Gilmartin, and Thomas Mellins. *New York 1930: Architecture and Urganism Between the Two World Wars.* New York, 1987.

Stern, Robert A. M., Thomas Mellins, and David Fishman. *New York 1960: Architecture and Urbanism Between the Second World War and the Bicentennial.* New York, 1995.

Stern, Robert A. M., Thomas Mellins and David Fishman. *New York 1880:, Architecture and Urbanism in the Gilded Age.* New York, 1990.

Stokes, I. N. Phelps. *The Iconography of Manhattan Island, 1498–1909 (6 vols).* New York, 1915–28.

Taborn, Karen. *Walking Harlem: The Ultimate Guide to the Cultural Capital of Black America.* New York, 2018.

Tauranac, John. *Elegant New York: The Builders and the Buildings 1885–1913.* New York, 1985.

___. *The Empire State Building: The Making of a Landmark.* New York, 1995.

Theodore, James, and Elizabeth Baker. *Fifth Avenue.* New York, 1971.

Tunick, Susan. *Terracotta Skyline: New York's Architectural Ornament.* New York, 1997.

van Rensselaer, M. G. "Fifth Avenue." *The Century Magazine,* 47 (November 1893): 5–18.

Wallace, Mike. *Greater Gotham: A History of New York City from 1898 to 1919.* New York, 2017.

White, Norval, Elliot Willensky, and Fran Leadon. *AIA Guide to New York City (5th Edition).* New York, 2010.

Willis, Carol. *Form Follows Finance: Skyscrapers and Skylines in New York and Chicago.* New York, 1995.

Wist, Ronda. *On Fifth Avenue: Then and Now.* New York, 1992.

Wright, Carol von Pressentin. *Blue Guide, New York (5th Edition).* New York, 2016.

Wright, Jennifer Nadler. *C .B .J. Snyder, New York City Public School Architecture, 1891–1922.* New York, 2020.

Helpful electronic resources include the official New York City landmark designation reports (https://www1.nyc.gov/site/lpc/designations/designation-reports.page) and the site "Every Building on Fifth Avenue" (https://landmarkbranding.com/blog/). Tom Miller's website "A Daytonian in Manhattan" in Manhattan is a fascinating source for information on individual buildings (http://daytoninmanhattan.blogspot.com/). Both the Bowery Boys website https://www.boweryboyshistory.com/ and Christopher Gray's long running "Streetscapes" columns in the *New York Times* are packed with information and insights. For the history of New York's department stores see: http://www.thedepartmentstoremuseum.org/2010/05/b-altman-co-new-york-city.html

Walking Fifth Avenue

Each of the six chapters in this book corresponds to a walk of about twenty to thirty blocks moving north up Fifth Avenue from Washington Square to Marcus Garvey Park at 120th Street and beyond through Central Harlem to the East River.

About fifty buildings are called out in each walk, usually identified by the name of the original or most notable owner and the street address. Buildings are numbered in the descriptions and illustrations, and these correspond to the numbering on the maps on the chapter openers.

Most chapters include at least one "detour" to explore buildings on the side streets extending east and west from Fifth Avenue itself. These pages are marked with an arrow and tinted in color.

The architectural history of Fifth Avenue (and all of Manhattan) is most easily read by looking up at the buildings. Most alterations for new uses, improved accessibility, or simply changing taste are made to the first two floors, and the original architecture is often intact on the upper floors.

Change is the only constant in New York. Buildings noted here as under construction or renovation will be unveiled and others will be shrouded in protective netting after this book is published.

Acknowledgments

While the observations, perceptions, and preferences in this book are my own, they are in good measure grounded in the research of others. I am deeply in these authors' debt. I am also grateful to the staffs of the Milstein and the Art and Architecture rooms at the New York Public Library, who have been uniformly welcoming and helpful. At Monacelli, editor Elizabeth White has been tireless in bringing shape and coherent form to the manuscript. She has kept me on my toes. She and her colleagues have produced a volume with the elgance and attention to detail characterisic of the publisher. Along the way I have benefitted from the unflagging support and encouragement of my friends and family. And there is simply no way to adequately thank my wife, Leslie, for the hundreds of hours and endless patience she devoted to editing, advising, nudging, and bucking up.

Photography Credits

Photographs by William J. Hennessey
except as noted below

Frederick Charles: 2
Mick Hales: 181
Larry Lederman: 90 below right
Library of Congress: 11, 15
Museum of the City of New York: 9 below, 12
New-York Historical Society: 9 top left
Office of Metropolitan History: 9 top right
OMA: 112 top
PBDW Architects: 115
Private Collection: 14
Max Touhey: Cover, 81
Jonathan Wallen: 21 left, 24 below, 30, 102, 148 top, 173 below
Samuel G. White: 55 below, 75 top left, 114 below left

Copyright © 2022 William J. Hennessey and The Monacelli Press,
a division of Phaidon Press, Inc.

First published in the United States in 2022. All rights reserved.

Library of Congress Control Number: 2022937722
ISBN 978-158093-607-1

Design: Shawn Hazen

Printed in China

Monacelli
A Phaidon Company
65 Bleecker Street
New York, New York 10012